21ST CENTURY COMMUNICATION
LISTENING, SPEAKING, AND CRITICAL THINKING

2

JESSICA WILLIAMS

Australia • Brazil • Mexico • Singapore • United Kingdom • United States

21st Century Communication: Listening,
Speaking, and Critical Thinking
Student Book 2
Jessica Williams

Publisher: Sherrise Roehr

Executive Editor: Laura Le Dréan

Managing Editor: Jennifer Monaghan

Senior Development Editor: Mary Whittemore

Associate Development Editor: Lisl Trowbridge

Media Research: Leila Hishmeh

Executive Marketing Manager: Ben Rivera

Product Marketing Manager: Anders Bylund

Sr. Director, Production: Michael Burggren

Manager, Production: Daisy Sosa

Content Project Manager: Mark Rzeszutek

Manufacturing Planner: Mary Beth Hennebury

Interior Design: Brenda Carmichael

Compositor: SPi Global

For product information and technology assistance, contact us at
Cengage Learning Customer & Sales Support, cengage.com/contact
For permission to use material from this text or product,
submit all requests online at **cengage.com/permissions**
Further permissions questions can be emailed to
permissionrequest@cengage.com

Student Book:
ISBN: 978-1-305-95545-5

Student Book with Online Workbook Sticker Code:
ISBN: 978-1-337-27581-1

National Geographic Learning
20 Channel Center Street
Boston, MA 02210
USA

National Geographic Learning, a Cengage Learning Company, has a mission to bring the world to the classroom and the classroom to life. With our English language programs, students learn about their world by experiencing it. Through our partnerships with National Geographic and TED, they develop the language and skills they need to be successful global citizens and leaders.

Cengage Learning is a leading provider of customized learning solutions with office locations around the globe, including Singapore, the United Kingdom, Australia, Mexico, Brazil, and Japan.

Cengage Learning products are represented in Canada by Nelson Education, Ltd.

Visit National Geographic Learning online at **ngl.cengage.com**

Visit our corporate website at **www.cengage.com**

Printed in the United States of America
Print Number: 03 Print Year: 2017

Reviewers

The author and publisher would like to thank the following teachers from all over the world for their valuable input during the development process of the *21st Century Communication* series.

Coleeta P. Abdullah, *EducationKSA, Saudi Arabia*

Ghada Al Attar, *AMIDEAST, Yemen*

Yazeed Al Jeddawy, *AMIDEAST, United Kingdom*

Zubidah Al Sallami, *AMIDEAST, Netherlands*

Ammar Al-Hawi, *AMIDEAST, Yemen*

William Albertson, *Drexel University English Language Center, Pennsylvania*

Tara Arntsen, *Northern State University, South Dakota*

Kevin Ballou, *Kobe College, Japan*

Nafisa Bintayeh, *AMIDEAST, Yemen*

Linda Bolet, *Houston Community College, Texas*

Tony Carnerie, *UCSD Extension, English Language Institute, California*

Catherine Cheetham, *Tokai University, Japan*

Celeste Coleman, *CSUSM American Language and Culture Institute, California*

Amy Cook, *Bowling Green State University, Ohio*

Katie Cottier, *University of Texas at Austin, Texas*

Teresita Curbelo, *Instituto Cultural Anglo Uruguayo, Uruguay*

Sarah de Pina, *ELS Boston Downtown, Massachusetts*

Rachel DeSanto, *Hillsborough Community College, Florida*

Silvana Dushku, *Intensive English Institute, Illinois*

Jennie Farnell, *University of Bridgeport, Connecticut*

Rachel Fernandez, *UCI Extension, International Programs, California*

Alayne Flores, *UCSD Extension, English Language Institute, California*

Claire Gimble, *Virginia International University, Virginia*

Floyd H. Graham III, *Kansai Gaidai University, Japan*

Kuei-ping Hsu, *National Tsing Hua University, Taiwan*

James Hughes, *Massachusetts International Academy / UMass Boston, Massachusetts*

Mariano Ignacio, *Centro Universitario de Idiomas, Argentina*

Jules L. Janse van Rensburg, *Chinese Culture University, South Africa*

Rachel Kadish, *GEOS Languages Plus Boston, Massachusetts*

Anthony Lavigne, *Kansai Gaidai University, Japan*

Ai-ping Liu, *National Central University Language Center, Taiwan*

Debra Liu, *City College of San Francisco, California*

Wilder Yesid Escobar Almeciga Imeciga, *Universidad El Bosque, Colombia*

Christina Lorimer, *SDSU American Language Institute, California*

Joanna Luper, *Liberty University, Virginia*

Joy MacFarland, *FLS Boston Commons, Massachusetts*

Elizabeth Mariscal, *UCSD Extension, English Language Institute, California*

Susan McAlister, *Language & Culture Center, University of Houston, Texas*

Wendy McBride, *Spring International Language Center at the University of Arkansas, Arkansas*

Monica McCrory, *University of Texas, Texas*

Katy Montgomery, *Purdue University, Indiana*

Katherine Murphy, *Massachusetts International Academy, Massachusetts*

Emily Naber, *Washington English Center, Washington*

Kavitha Nambisan, *University of Tennessee-Martin, Tennessee*

Sandra Navarro, *Glendale Community College, California*

Fernanda Ortiz, *Center for English as a Second Language at the University of Arizona, Arizona*

Pamela Patterson, *Seminole State College, Florida*

Grace Pimcias, *CSUSM American Language and Culture Institute, California*

Jennie Popp, *Universidad Andres Bello, Chile*

Jamie Reinstein, *Community College of Philadelphia, Pennsylvania*

Philip Rice, *University of Delaware, Delaware*

Helen Roland, *Miami Dade College, Florida*

Yoko Sakurai, *Aichi University, Japan*

Jenay Seymour, *Hongik University (Sejong Campus), South Korea*

Margaret Shippey, *Miami Dade College, Florida*

William Slade, *University of Texas at Austin, Texas*

Kelly Smith, *UCSD Extension, English Language Institute, California*

Rachel Stokes, *University of Texas at Austin, Texas*

Joshua Stone, *Approach International Student Center, Massachusetts*

Judy Tanka, *UCLA Extension, California*

Mary M. Wang, *University of Wisconsin-Madison, Wisconsin*

Judy Wong, *Pace University, New York*

Scope and Sequence

PRONUNCIATION SKILL	NOTE-TAKING SKILL	TED TALKS	PRESENTATION SKILL	UNIT ASSIGNMENT
Stress content words	Use an outline	*Half a million secrets* **Frank Warren**	Start strong	Give a group presentation about how people in your community can share their hopes, thoughts, and ideas
Reduced vowels	Use short phrases	*How I swam the North Pole* **Lewis Pugh**	Make an emotional connection	Give an individual presentation about an environmental or social topic that is important to you
Can and *can't*	Make a time line	*Happy maps* **Daniele Quercia**	Pause	Give an individual presentation on your own happy map
Numbers	Review your notes	*Forget shopping. Soon you'll download your new clothes.* **Danit Peleg**	Prepare for an interview	Work with a partner to interview a classmate about his or her opinions on recent fashion trends
Linking sounds	Take notes using key terms	*Why I make robots the size of a grain of rice* **Sarah Bergbreiter**	Have a strong ending	Give a group presentation about other applications for biomimicry projects
Speak in thought groups	Use symbols	*Should you donate differently?* **Joy Sun**	Be personable	Participate in a role play about how to donate money to people in need
Intonation in *yes/no* and choice questions	Record information in a list	*Less stuff, more happiness* **Graham Hill**	Connect the ending to the beginning	Give a group presentation about the topic, "less is more"
Intonation in *wh-* questions	Use mind maps	*A drone's-eye view of conservation* **Lian Pin Koh**	Use visuals effectively	Give a group presentation about an animal that is under threat

1 Half a million secrets
FRANK WARREN

2 How I swam the North Pole
LEWIS PUGH

3 Happy maps
DANIELE QUERCIA

4 Forget shopping. Soon you'll
download your new clothes.
DANIT PELEG

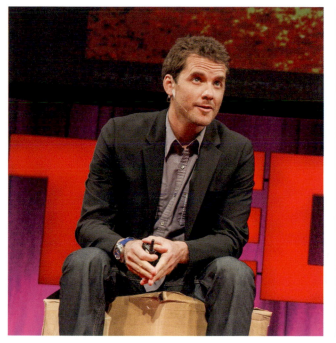

Welcome to 21st Century Communication

21st Century Communication: Listening, Speaking, and Critical Thinking develops essential listening, speaking, and presentation skills to help learners succeed with their academic and professional goals. Students learn key academic skills as they engage with thought-provoking TED Talks and 21st century themes and skills such as global awareness, information literacy, and critical thinking.

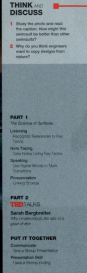

Each unit opens with an impactful photograph related to a **21st century theme** and Think and Discuss questions to draw students into the topic.

Part 1 introduces a variety of **listening inputs** including lectures, interviews, podcasts, and classroom discussions. Selected listenings are accompanied by video slide shows.

Listening, speaking, note-taking, and pronunciation skills are explicitly taught and practiced. Woven throughout are 21st century skills of **collaboration, communication,** and **critical thinking.**

Part 2 introduces the TED speaker and the idea
worth spreading. Students explore and discuss
the ideas while at the same time seamlessly
applying the skills learned in Part 1.

Real-world infographics engage
students more deeply with the unit
theme and promote **visual literacy**.

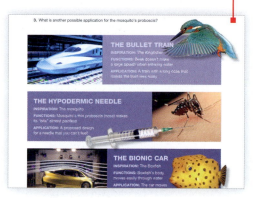

Presentation Skills
inspired by the TED
speakers give students
the skills and authentic
language they need
to successfully
deliver their own
presentations.

Put It Together helps students **connect
ideas** and prepares them for their
final assignment. Students synthesize
information and consolidate their learning.

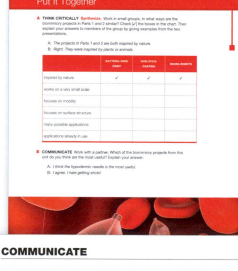

Reflect encourages
students to **take
charge of their
learning**, another
21st century skill.

Fully blended **Online Workbooks powered by
MyELT** help develop **digital literacy skills** by
offering students the complete audio and video
program along with speech-recognition and auto-
graded language practice activities.

Secret Wishes

In Bhutan, two boys share a secret.

THINK AND DISCUSS

1 Look at the photo. What are the children doing? What do you think they are telling secrets about?

2 Read the title. Would you share your secret wishes with anyone? Who? Why would you choose that person?

BEFORE YOU LISTEN

A COMMUNICATE Work in small groups. Discuss these questions.

1. Look at the photo and read the information in the box and the caption. Do you think Chang's neighbors will complete the statements? Why, or why not?

2. Do you have a list of things you'd like to do before you die? Have you ever told anyone what's on the list? Why, or why not?

B THINK CRITICALLY **Predict.** What topics do you think people will write about on Chang's wall? Rank the topics with *1* being the most popular and *6* being the least popular. Then discuss your answers in a small group.

_____ Fame	_____ Love	_____ Travel
_____ Happiness	_____ Money	_____ Work

Hopes And Dreams

In 2011, artist Candy Chang started a community art project. She wanted people in her neighborhood in New Orleans to share their hopes and dreams. She wrote one sentence on a wall over and over again: *Before I die, I want to* _____. She waited to see how her neighbors would complete the sentence.

Candy Chang starts her project on an empty building in New Orleans, U.S.

VOCABULARY

C 🎧 **1.2** Read and listen to the statements with words from the class discussion you will hear. Guess the meaning of each bold word. Then match each word to its definition.

a. I was surprised by some of the **responses** that people wrote on the wall.

b. This is a very **private** issue, so I don't talk about it with other people very often.

c. She is very shy and does not like to speak **in public.**

d. He is **depressed** because his mother is really sick and his father died just a few months ago.

e. Some of the responses were kind of **silly.** For example, one person just wanted to eat a lot of chocolate.

f. Other responses seemed a bit **selfish.** For example, one person wanted a big boat. Another person wanted to live in a house that cost $500,000.

g. It is really **heartbreaking** to see houses in the neighborhood falling down and my neighbors moving away. It makes me very sad.

h. We have neighborhood parties in the summer, which help bring everyone in the **community** together.

i. If you like the idea of leaving messages on a wall, you can start a **similar** wall in your own community.

j. After she collected **data** from all the walls in all of the different countries, she realized there were more than 100,000 responses!

1. _____ (n) all of the people in one group or area

2. _____ (n) information

3. _____ (adj) very unhappy

4. _____ (adj) causing great sadness

5. _____ (phrase) where anyone can see or hear

6. _____ (adj) personal, for just one person

7. _____ (n) answers

8. _____ (adj) caring only about yourself

9. _____ (adj) not serious

10. _____ (adj) almost the same

D **COMMUNICATE** Work with a partner. Give examples of each of the following. Then explain your answers to your partner using the words in bold.

> A: *Have you helped your* **community***?*
> B: *Yes, I help an older neighbor in my* **community** *with his grocery shopping.*

1. **Data** that should be kept **private**

2. **Silly** behavior

3. Something you have done to help your **community**

4. A **heartbreaking** news story

5. **Selfish** behavior

LISTEN

E 🎧 **1.3** **LISTEN FOR MAIN IDEAS** Listen to the class discussion. Choose the best phrase to complete each main idea from the discussion.

1. Chang started the project because _____ .

   a. she was feeling unhappy

   b. she wanted to make her neighborhood more attractive

   c. she knew the wall would be popular

2. When the students considered the responses on all the walls, they realized that many of the topics were _____ .

   a. about helping other people

   b. about making people smile

   c. depressing

3. The walls _____ .

   a. are only in poorer neighborhoods

   b. help people connect with each other

   c. allow people to meet with friends

learnmore New Orleans, Candy Chang's hometown, was devastated by Hurricane Katrina in 2005. Many neighborhoods were badly damaged and around 40% of the population was forced to leave.

LISTENING SKILL Recognize Examples

Speakers often include examples to illustrate their ideas. Listening for examples can help you better understand and remember these ideas. Listen for the following phrases that speakers use to introduce examples:

for example . . .   for instance . . .   such as . . .

like . . .   an example of . . .

Sometimes speakers give examples without using an introductory phrase:

"A chapter at the end of the Chang's book gives some data about the responses. Nineteen percent of the responses were about love."

Speakers may also use photos or other visuals to introduce their examples.

NOTE-TAKING SKILL Use an Outline

Using an outline can help you take notes that are clearly organized. In English, a good outline starts with an important idea on the left. Then supporting examples related to the idea are added underneath and indented.

Idea 1

    Example 1

    Example 2

Idea 2

    Example 1

    Example 2

F 🎧 **1.4** **LISTEN FOR EXAMPLES** Listen to segment 1 of the discussion. Use the outline to complete the notes. Pay attention to phrases that introduce each example.

Idea 1: Helping people and making the world better

    Example: _____ **I want to help a million people** _____ .
                                              1

    Example: _____ .
                                            2

Idea 2: Things people wanted for themselves

    Example: _____ .
                                            3

    Example: _____ .
                                            4

Idea 3: Love and happiness

    Example: _____ .
                                            5

    Example: _____ .
                                            6

Idea 4: Travel

    Example: _____ .
                                            7

    Example: _____ .
                                          8

Local resident Adam Kampe writes on a *Before I Die* ... wall in Washington, D.C.

G 🎧 **1.5** **LISTEN FOR DETAILS** Listen to segment 2. Choose the best word or phrase to complete each statement.

1. Over _____ *Before I Die* ... walls have been created around the world.

    a. 100   **b.** 1,000   **c.** 1,500

2. Mateo thinks people write on walls because _____ .

    a. it feels sad and painful

    b. it makes them feel better

    c. they are popular

3. Mika believes that the walls _____ .

    a. make people happy

    b. are good for shy people

    c. bring people together

4. Ana probably _____ .

    a. would not write a response on a wall

    b. agrees with Mika

    c. understands the purpose of the walls

AFTER YOU LISTEN

H THINK CRITICALLY **Interpret an Infographic.** Work with a partner. The infographic shows an analysis of the responses on thousands of *Before I Die …* walls. Study the chart. Then answer the questions.

1. The chart categorizes _____ responses on *Before I Die …* walls.

   a. different kinds of   **b.** the most common words used in   **c.** Chang's favorite

2. Write the three most frequent topics of the responses on the walls.

   a. _____   **b.** _____   **c.** _____

3. Why do you think so many of the responses are about these three topics?

4. How do the most frequent topics from the student discussion compare with the most frequent topics on *all* of the walls? Are they exactly the same? Or are some topics different?

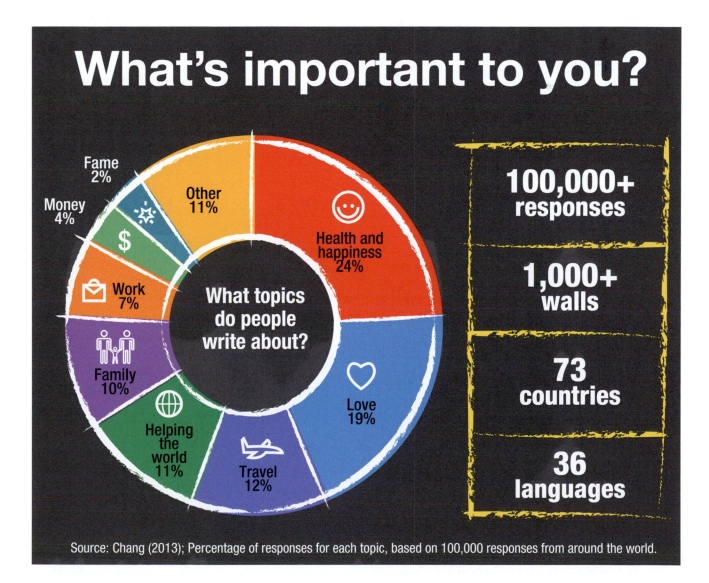

What's important to you?

What topics do people write about?

- Fame 2%
- Money 4%
- Other 11%
- Work 7%
- Family 10%
- Helping the world 11%
- Travel 12%
- Love 19%
- Health and happiness 24%

100,000+ responses

1,000+ walls

73 countries

36 languages

Source: Chang (2013); Percentage of responses for each topic, based on 100,000 responses from around the world.

I THINK CRITICALLY Apply. Work with a small group. The professor sent an email that included all the students' favorite *Before I Die …* responses. Discuss how you would categorize each response using the topics from the chart in exercise H. More than one answer is possible.

> A: *I think "go to the moon" is about travel.*
> B: *Yes. It could also be about fame!*

To   All students

Subject   Your favorite Chang responses

Dear class—here are the responses you liked best from Candy Chang's *Before I Die …* project.

Before I die, I want to …

- go to the moon.
- play football with Messi.
- work at Google.
- have an honest conversation with my mother.
- make a difference in someone's life.
- quit smoking.
- be a successful artist.
- have peace in my country.
- get a good score on the TOEFL.

SPEAKING

During a discussion, speakers often use phrases to show they agree or disagree with another speaker.

Use these phrases to agree:

I agree.   *True.*   *Good point.*   *Exactly.*   *Absolutely.*
I was just about to say that.

Use these phrases to disagree and to introduce your own opinion.

I disagree.   *I don't know.*   *I don't think so.*
I'm not so sure (about that).

A: *Most people want to help others.*

B: ***I am not so sure about that.*** *A lot of people want to help themselves.*

J 🎧 **1.6** Work with a partner. Listen to the following statements and responses from the discussion. Choose *agree* or *disagree* and write the phrase that is used. Then compare your answers with a partner.

1. Mateo: *"I think people write on the walls because it makes them feel better."*

   Mika agrees/~~disagrees~~. She uses the phrase _____I'm not so sure_____.

2. Mika: *"The wall lets you talk to everyone and listen to everyone."*

   The professor agrees/disagrees. He uses the phrase _____.

3. Mateo: *"Sharing our feelings with others makes us feel better, but it also builds connections among people in the community."*

   The professor agrees/disagrees. He uses the phrase _____.

4. Mika: *"The wall builds those connections with people we don't even know."*

   Ana agrees/disagrees. She uses the phrase _____.

5. Mateo: *"The walls are popular because sometimes it is easier to share them in public with strangers."*

   The professor agrees/disagrees. He uses the phrase _____.

K **THINK CRITICALLY Apply.** Take a class survey. Follow the steps.

1. What topic would you write about on a *Before I Die …* wall?

2. Write the topic on a piece of paper. Don't write your name.

3. Choose one or two students to collect the results, group them, and present to the class.

4. Discuss the results. Are the class results similar to the results in the infographic on page 9? If so, why do you think so? If not, why do you think they are different?

PRONUNCIATION SKILL Stress Content Words

Speakers stress content words by saying them louder and more clearly than other words. Content words are nouns, verbs, adjectives, adverbs, and the negative *no/not*. They contain the most important information in a sentence.*

Listen to the following sentence and notice the stressed content words.

1.7 *"**Chang** was **feel**ing **ve**ry un**hap**py because a **friend** had **died.**"*
　　　　N　　　V　　　Adv　　Adj　　　　　　N　　　　V

*If a content word has more than one syllable, just one of the syllables is usually stressed.

L **1.8** Work in a group of three. Label each bold content word (N, V, Adj, Adv, Neg) in the excerpt. Then listen and notice the stressed words.

> Ana: *"I **don't really** under**stand** why **peo**ple want to **share** these **pri**vate **feel**ings*
> 　　　　Neg
>
> *with **stran**gers."*

> Mateo: *"**That**'s my **point**. The **walls** are **pop**ular because sometimes it is **ea**sier to*
>
> ***share** them in **pub**lic with **stran**gers."*

> Professor: *"**That**'s a **good point**, Mateo."*

M With your group, practice the conversation from exercise L. Take turns saying each part. Be sure to stress the content words as indicated.

N **COMMUNICATE** Work with a partner. Discuss the statements below. Begin your responses with phrases that show you agree or disagree. Be sure to stress content words. Be prepared to explain your responses.

> A: *Most neighbors don't talk to each other any more.*
>
> B: *I don't know. The people in my neighborhood are very friendly and helpful.*

1. Neighbors don't talk to each other as much as in the past.

2. Walls like Chang's are not the best way to connect people in a community.

3. It is important to set goals for yourself when you are young.

Half a million secrets

> 66 [Secrets] can connect us with our deepest humanity. 99

BEFORE YOU WATCH

A COMMUNICATE Work with a partner. Read the title and information about the TED speaker. What do you think happened after he handed out the postcards?

FRANK WARREN   Secret Keeper

Frank Warren is the creator of the community art project, PostSecret.com, a Web site where people can share their secrets. He has published five books about the secrets he collected on the Web site.

Warren's project began as a small experiment in 2004. He handed out blank postcards to people on the street. Warren asked people to write something on the postcard that they'd never told anyone before and mail the postcards back to him. He didn't know what to expect.

Frank Warren's idea worth spreading is that sharing secrets can help us connect with others and know ourselves better.

B COMMUNICATE Read the following statements and check [✓] the ones that you agree with. Then tell a partner which items you agree with and why.

> A: *I don't think it is a good idea to share secrets.*
> B: *Really? Why?*
> A: *Because someone could get hurt.*

1. ☐ Some secrets should never be shared.

2. ☐ It's easier to share a secret with someone you don't know very well.

3. ☐ Sharing secrets can make people feel better.

VOCABULARY

C 🎧 **1.9** The sentences below will help you learn words in the TED Talk. Read and listen to the sentences. Guess the meaning of each bold word. Then complete each sentence with the correct word.

a. The competition organizer chose a winner **randomly** from thousands of entries.

b. The suicide note was really **shocking**. We could not believe that she wanted to take her own life.

c. He has received **countless** postcards and emails about his project. He stopped counting them after the first thousand.

d. You can call or write **anonymously** and give your opinion. You do not have to give your name.

e. We want to **preserve** the beautiful old homes in our community. If we do not, they will disappear.

f. The handwriting on these two postcards is **obviously** very different. You can see this difference right away.

g. The class project really allowed students to demonstrate their **creativity**. Some students drew pictures and others wrote poems about their neighborhood.

h. After the fire, the **remains** of the home were just a few burned pieces of furniture.

i. A neighbor ran into the burning house and saved the children. The community praised her **heroism**.

j. This whole community arts project was an experiment. We did not know how it would **play out**.

1. We listened to the _____ announcement about the young singer's death.

2. The police officer received an award for _____ after she saved a boy's life.

3. Many people come to visit the artist's house, which _____ the spirit of his life and work.

4. The teacher called on students _____ to answer questions. She did not go in any order.

5. We will just have to wait and see how this plan _____. Maybe it will be successful, and maybe it will fail.

6. The teacher was pleased by the _____ of his students' artwork.

7. We _____ have to review the plans again. No one understands them at all.

8. There have been _____ attempts to solve the problem, but none of them has succeeded so far.

9. We vote for the president _____. No one will know what your vote was.

10. The _____ of the last night's dinner were still on the table when we woke up this morning.

D COMMUNICATE Work with a partner. Discuss these questions. Use the words in bold in your answers.

    A: *What kind of jobs require **creativity**?*
    B: *Definitely an artist.*

1. What kinds of jobs require **creativity?**

2. What kinds of jobs require **heroism?**

3. What do most people do when they hear something **shocking?**

4. Do you think people should be allowed to comment **anonymously** on Web sites? Or do you think they should have to give their names?

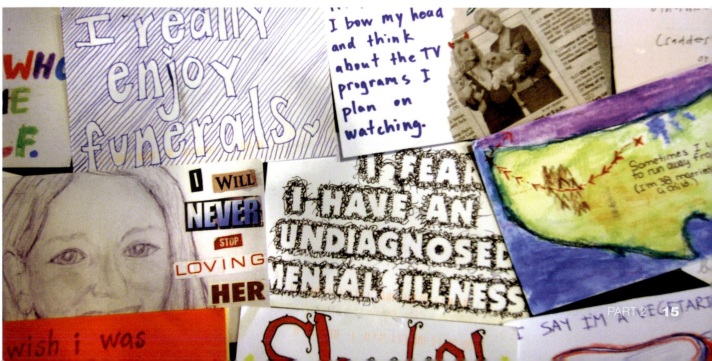

WATCH

E ▶ **1.1** **WATCH FOR DETAILS** Watch segment 1 of Warren's edited TED Talk. Complete the summary below.

Frank Warren created ___*3000*___ postcards. On the postcards,
                                        1

he asked people to share a ___*secret*___ that they had never told anyone
                                            2

before. He handed the postcards out to strangers in _____. The
                                                                    3

idea spread virally. People began to ___*buy*___ and make their own
                                                    4

postcards. Soon his idea didn't seem so ___*crazy*___.
                                                        5

F ▶ **1.2** **WATCH FOR MAIN IDEAS** Watch segment 2 of Warren's edited TED Talk. Check [✓] the statement that best expresses the main idea.

1. ☐ The success of PostSecret.com was a surprise.

2. ☑ Secrets can be powerful.

3. ☐ Warren started the project because he liked secrets.

G **THINK CRITICALLY** **Infer.** Read the excerpt from the talk. What is Warren trying to say? Check [✓] the best interpretation.

"Secrets can take many forms. They can be silly or soulful or shocking. They can connect us with our deepest humanity or with people we'll never meet again. … Secrets can remind us of the countless human dramas of frailty and heroism, playing out silently in the lives of people all around us even now."

1. ☐ Our secrets are all very similar.

2. ☐ Secrets should be spoken quietly.

3. ☐ People have many different kinds of secrets.

H ▶ **1.2 RECOGNIZE EXAMPLES** Watch segment 2 again. Listen and watch for examples that support Warren's main idea. Complete the outline below.

Idea: Secrets can take many forms. They can be silly, soulful, or shocking.

- *"I found these stamps as a child, and I have been waiting all my life to have someone to send them to. I never* ___*did*___ *."*
- *"I give decaf to people who are* ___*never*___ *to me."*
  ₁
- *"Dear Birthmother, I have great parents. I've found* ___*love*___ *. I'm*
  ₂
  ___*Kom happy*___ *."*
  ₃
  ₄
- *"Inside this envelope is the ripped up remains of a suicide note I didn't use. I feel like the* ___*~~p~~ happiest person*___ *on Earth (now)."*
  ₅
- *"When people I love leave voicemails on my phone, I always save them in case they die tomorrow and I have no other way of hearing* ___*their voice*___ *ever again."*
  ₆

I THINK CRITICALLY Infer. Choose the best word or phrase to complete each statement. Then compare your answers with a partner's.

1. The person who wrote the postcard about the stamps is probably _____.

   a. worried   **b.** angry   **c.** unhappy

2. The writer gave the customers decaf coffee because s/he _____.

   a. was mad at them   **b.** knew they wanted decaf   **c.** didn't care

3. The sender of the "birthmother" postcard probably _____ his/her biological mother.

   a. met   **b.** does not know   **c.** will find

4. The writer who sent a ripped up suicide note probably _____ in the past.

   a. was successful   **b.** was happier   **c.** had a lot of problems

5. The person who sent the song wanted to _____.

   a. celebrate a birthday   **b.** share a secret   **c.** remember someone

---

WORDS IN THE TALK
birthmother (n): biological mother of a child who was adopted by other people
decaf (n): coffee that does not wake you up
frailty (n): weakness
humanity (n): understanding and kindness toward other people
soulful (adj): full of feeling

J ▶ **1.3** **EXPAND YOUR VOCABULARY** Watch the excerpts from the TED Talk. Guess the meanings of the phrases in the box.

> hand out   spreading virally   a handful of   does a great job of   in case

K **WATCH MORE** Go to TED.com to watch the full TED Talk by Frank Warren.

AFTER YOU WATCH

L **COMMUNICATE** Work in a small group. What kinds of secrets did Warren reveal in his TED Talk? Complete the mind map below with these examples of secrets from his talk. Write the numbers in the mind map. More than one answer may be possible. Use phrases to agree or disagree.

1. The "stamps" secret
2. The "Starbucks" secret
3. The "birthmother" secret

4. The "suicide" secret
5. The "voicemail" secret

A: *The Starbucks postcard is an example of a silly secret.*

B: *I agree.*

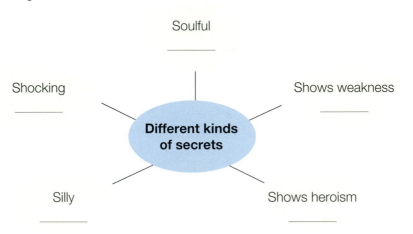

M **THINK CRITICALLY** **Reflect.** Work with a small group. Discuss your answers to these questions.

1. Warren says that sharing secrets can be "powerful." Do you agree? Explain your answer.

2. Do you think there could be a negative side to sharing secrets with strangers? Give some examples.

3. Would you share a secret on PostSecret.com? Why, or why not?

Put It Together

A THINK CRITICALLY Synthesize. Work with a group. How are Candy Chang's and Frank Warren's projects similar? In what ways are they different? Discuss the questions and complete the chart with information from Parts 1 and 2.

	BEFORE I DIE ... WALL	POSTSECRET.COM
Why did Chang and Warren start these projects?	To connect to the community	
How do the people communicate their messages in these projects?		
What kinds of ideas and messages do people share?		
What is the effect on the people who share the hopes and secrets?		
What is the effect of the project on people who read the messages?		

B THINK CRITICALLY Apply. Why do you think that people feel comfortable sharing their wishes and secrets in these ways? Explain your answer. What makes you feel comfortable or safe enough to share your wishes or secrets?

COMMUNICATE

ASSIGNMENT: Group Presentation Your group is going to give a presentation about how people in your community can share their hopes, thoughts, and ideas.

PREPARE

PRESENTATION SKILL Start Strong

The beginning of a good presentation gets—and holds—the attention of the audience. A speaker can make a strong start by telling a surprising story, giving a quote or interesting example, asking a challenging question, or showing a powerful picture. A strong start makes the audience think and makes them want to know what comes next.

▶ **1.4** Watch this excerpt from the talk. Notice how Warren starts his talk.

"Hi, my name is Frank, and I collect secrets. It all started with a crazy idea in November of 2004. I printed up 3,000 self-addressed postcards, just like this. They were blank on one side, and on the other side I listed some simple instructions."

C Work with your group. Complete the presentation outline below. Use the class discussion in Part 1, the TED Talk in Part 2, and your own ideas.

1. What statement would you ask people in your community to complete? Add a few of your own ideas. Choose one.

☐ I hope other people will _____ .

☐ My dream is to _____ .

☐ Our community needs _____ .

☐ [Your ideas] _____ .

_____ .

2. How would people share their messages? Choose one.

☐ On a wall

☐ On a postcard

☐ On a Web site

☐ [Your idea] _____

A sign encourages people to post notes about their New Year's resolutions in London, England.

D COLLABORATE In your group, decide who will do the following tasks in your presentation.

- Introduce the presentation. Remember to **start strong** and **stress content words.** Will you . . .
  - tell a story?
  - give an example?
  - show a picture?
  - ask a question?
- Explain your project.
  - Explain the purpose of your project and say why it is meaningful.
  - Share the statement that you chose and explain why you chose it.
  - State how people will share their messages.
  - Give an example of a message that someone might share.
- Give a short conclusion about why you think this project will be helpful to your community.

E Read the rubric on page 179. Notice how your presentation will be evaluated. Keep these categories in mind as you present and watch your classmates' presentations.

PRESENT

F Give your group presentation to the class. Watch your classmates' presentations.

G THINK CRITICALLY Evaluate. Discuss your evaluations and feedback in a small group. Decide the two things you did well and two areas for improvement.

REFLECT

Reflect on what you have learned. Check [✓] your progress.

I can
- ☐ recognize supporting examples.
- ☐ use an outline.
- ☐ use phrases to agree or disagree with another speaker.
- ☐ stress content words.
- ☐ start strong when giving a presentation.

I understand the meanings of these words and can use them.
Circle those you know. Underline those you need to work on.

anonymously	depressed AWL	play out	response AWL
community AWL	heartbreaking	preserve	selfish
countless	heroism	private	shocking
creativity AWL	in public	randomly AWL	silly
data AWL	obviously AWL	remains	similar AWL

Changing Climate, Changing Minds

1 Read the unit title and study the photo. How is the world's climate changing? What does "changing minds" mean in this context?

2 Who or what do you think is affected by climate change?

Giant pieces of sea ice washed up on a beach in Iceland.

PART 1 Land Underwater!

BEFORE YOU LISTEN

A COMMUNICATE Work with a partner. Look at the photo and read the caption and the information in the box. Then discuss these questions.

1. What has happened to the Arctic sea ice since 1979?

2. What might be the effect of rising sea levels in the Maldives?

Melting Ice, Rising Waters

The world's average temperature is rising. The higher temperature causes sea ice to melt. This melted ice runs into the oceans and causes the sea level to rise. Higher sea levels lead to more frequent floods and more dangerous storms along the coasts.

1979
2.78

**Arctic ice, average
September extent**
in million square miles

2015
1.79

Sources: Jennifer Frances, Rutgers University; Dennis Hartmann, University of Washington

The Maldives, a chain of over 1,000 islands in the Indian Ocean, is a popular tourist destination.

VOCABULARY

B 🎧 **1.10** Read and listen to the sentences with words from the student presentation you will hear. Guess the meanings of the words in bold. Then complete each sentence below with the correct word.

a. Before the flooding, government leaders did not believe that climate change was real. Now, they are finally **taking** it **seriously**.

b. Some cities have already made plans for climate change. Unfortunately, other cities have **barely** started their preparations. They need to do more now.

c. Sea walls can give cities on the coast some **protection** against floods.

d. Scientists **predict** that by the year 2100, the sea level will rise by up to five feet.

e. One city with no natural lakes has built an **artificial** lake. The new lake can hold a lot of rainwater during heavy storms.

f. You can read about climate change in **documents** prepared by the United Nations.

g. Many countries agreed to reduce pollution, but without a plan of action it was mainly a **symbolic** gesture.

h. Loss of sea ice has dangerous **consequences**, such as more frequent floods.

i. There has been a **dramatic** increase in the number of floods in the last 10 years—up 50 percent.

j. At the **current** rate of increase, there will be more floods in the future.

1. The speaker has a soft voice so we can _____ hear her.

2. You should keep important _____ , such as your passport, in a safe place.

3. The photographs are not worth a lot of money, but they have great _____ importance.

4. Experts _____ that the world's population will be 9.7 billion in 2050.

5. He spends four hours every night on his homework. He is _____ his schoolwork very _____ this semester.

6. There was a(n) _____ change in the price of oil in 2008. It fell from $145 to $30 in less than six months.

7. Any increase in the price of oil will have serious _____ for the whole country.

8. I use only real sugar in my coffee. I don't like the _____ kind.

9. The _____ temperature is 68 degrees F, but it will get warmer later today.

10. The police provide _____ for everyone in the city.

C **COMMUNICATE** Work with a partner. Take turns asking and answering the questions. Use the words in bold in your answers.

1. Have there been any **dramatic** changes in your country in the last 10 years? Explain.

2. What have the **consequences** of these changes been?

3. What do you **predict** will happen in your life in the next five years?

4. What is something that you **take** very **seriously**?

5. What objects have **symbolic** importance for you or your family?

LISTEN

D 🎧 **1.11** ▶ **1.5** **LISTEN FOR MAIN IDEAS** Read the statements below. Then listen to the student presentation. Write T for *true*, F for *false*, or N for *not mentioned*.

1. _____ Climate change has affected the Maldives more than other countries.

2. _____ The situation in the Maldives could happen to other countries in the future.

3. _____ The Maldives has not had a flood since the 2004 tsunami.

4. _____ Many coastal areas in Asia could be flooded by rising sea levels in the future.

5. _____ Most of the world's ice will probably melt by 2100.

WORDS IN THE PRESENTATION
tsunami (n): a large and dangerous wave caused by an earthquake under the ocean

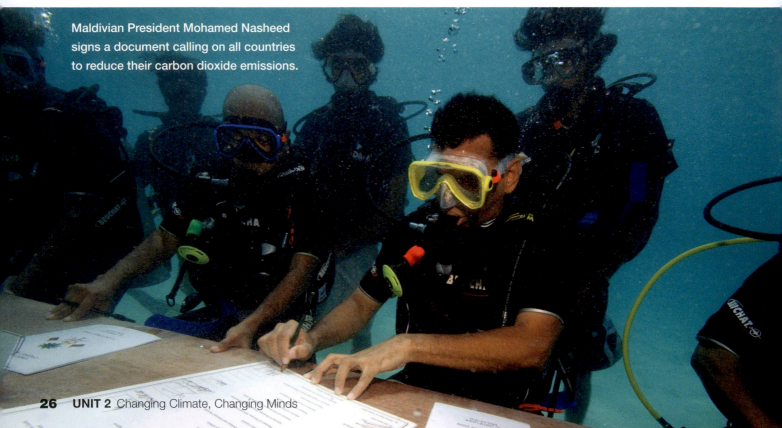

Maldivian President Mohamed Nasheed signs a document calling on all countries to reduce their carbon dioxide emissions.

LISTENING SKILL Listen for Details

Speakers often provide details about an event by including more information about where, when, how, or why something happened. Other details include information about who and what were involved. Listening for these details can help you understand more about the speaker's ideas.

Where: Listen for names of places (e.g., the Maldives).

When: Listen for dates (e.g., 2004).

Who: Listen for names of people (e.g., President Nasheed).

How many: Listen for numbers (e.g., five feet).

What: Listen for things (e.g., sea levels).

(See page 163 in the *Independent Student Handbook* for more information on listening for details.)

E 🎧 **1.12 LISTEN FOR DETAILS** In the presentation, the student described three steps the Maldives government took after the 2004 tsunami. Listen to segment 2 of the student presentation and complete the details in the mind map below.

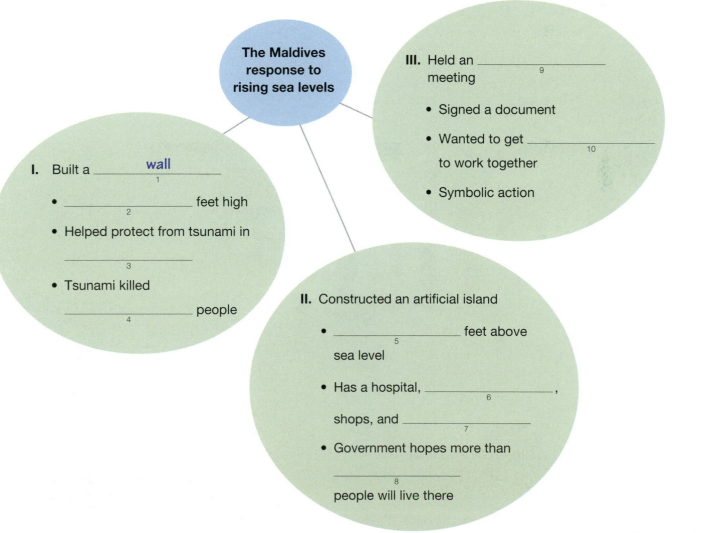

The Maldives response to rising sea levels

I. Built a ___wall___ (1)

- _____ feet high (2)
- Helped protect from tsunami in _____ (3)
- Tsunami killed _____ people (4)

II. Constructed an artificial island

- _____ feet above (5) sea level
- Has a hospital, _____ (6), shops, and _____ (7)
- Government hopes more than _____ (8) people will live there

III. Held an _____ (9) meeting

- Signed a document
- Wanted to get _____ (10) to work together
- Symbolic action

F 🎧 **1.13 LISTEN FOR DETAILS** Listen to segment 3 of the student presentation. Then complete the sentences with the correct numbers.

1. If all of the world's sea ice melts, scientists say the sea level could rise by _____ feet.

2. In China, _____ million people would be made homeless.

3. Scientists predict that if it continues at the current rate, the earth's sea ice could melt in the next _____ years.

AFTER YOU LISTEN

G **THINK CRITICALLY Analyze.** Work with a small group. Discuss these questions.

1. At the start of the presentation, the presenter asks "*Why aren't we taking climate change more seriously?*" Check [✓] what you think was the main purpose of her presentation.
   a. ☐ to describe the effects of climate change in the Maldives
   b. ☐ to persuade her audience that climate change has consequences today
   c. ☐ to explain how we can prevent a future rise in the sea level

2. Do you agree that people are getting tired of the topic of climate change? Why might that be so?

3. Are you tired of hearing about climate change? What was your reaction to the presentation?

Mohamed Shaheed, an administrator of the Hulhumale project, shows a model of what the artificial island may look like once it is completed.

SPEAKING

When speaking, it is often necessary to describe the causes and effects of an event or action. This helps listeners understand how or why the event or action is important. For example, the cause of melting sea ice is climate change. One effect of sea ice melt is an increase in sea levels.

Notice how the words and phrases to signal cause and effect are used in the following examples:

Cause		Effect
Climate change	***causes***	*sea ice to melt.*
The loss of sea ice	***leads to***	*an increase in sea level.*
Climate change has had an	***effect/impact***	*on sea ice.*

Effect		Cause
Sea levels are rising	***because***	*the sea ice is melting.*
More sea ice will melt	***as a result of***	*climate change.*

(See page 165 in the *Independent Student Handbook* for more information on talking about causes and effects.)

H **COLLABORATE** Work with a partner. Complete the cause and effect chain by putting the events in the correct order. Then use signal words and phrases of cause and effect to describe these events to your partner.

> A: *One effect of climate change is higher sea levels.*
> B: *Right. And higher sea levels have led to more floods and storms.*

1. **a.** more floods and storms
   b. higher sea levels
   c. climate change

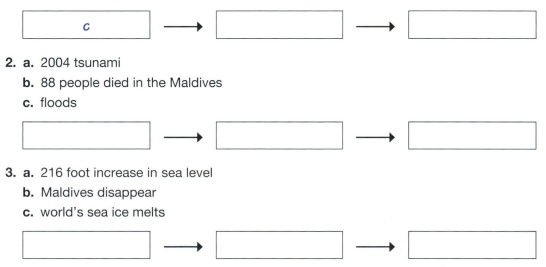

| c | → | | → | |

2. **a.** 2004 tsunami
   b. 88 people died in the Maldives
   c. floods

| | → | | → | |

3. **a.** 216 foot increase in sea level
   b. Maldives disappear
   c. world's sea ice melts

| | → | | → | |

I   THINK CRITICALLY   Interpret an Infographic. Work with a partner. Look at the infographic and read the captions. Then discuss your answers to these questions.

1. Where is the sea level likely to rise the most by the year 2100?

2. What do you think *exposed assets* means?

3. Which two cities would have the greatest economic losses?

4. Where might the most people be in danger?

J Work with a small group. Choose three of the cities on the map. What could happen to them by 2100? Explain to your group. Use phrases to show cause and effect.

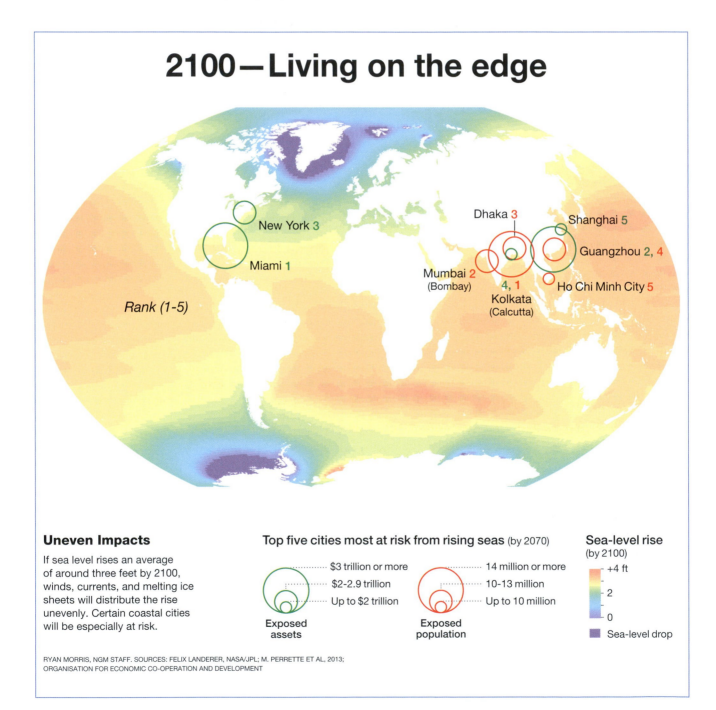

2100—Living on the edge

New York 3

Miami 1

Dhaka 3

Shanghai 5

Guangzhou 2, 4

Mumbai 2
(Bombay)

4, 1

Ho Chi Minh City 5

Kolkata
(Calcutta)

Rank (1-5)

Uneven Impacts

If sea level rises an average of around three feet by 2100, winds, currents, and melting ice sheets will distribute the rise unevenly. Certain coastal cities will be especially at risk.

Top five cities most at risk from rising seas (by 2070)

- $3 trillion or more
- $2-2.9 trillion
- Up to $2 trillion

Exposed assets

- 14 million or more
- 10-13 million
- Up to 10 million

Exposed population

Sea-level rise
(by 2100)

- +4 ft
- 2
- 0
- Sea-level drop

RYAN MORRIS, NGM STAFF. SOURCES: FELIX LANDERER, NASA/JPL; M. PERRETTE ET AL, 2013; ORGANISATION FOR ECONOMIC CO-OPERATION AND DEVELOPMENT

PRONUNCIATION SKILL Reduced Vowels

Speakers often reduce the vowels in these types of words:

Prepositions (e.g., *of, on*)

Indefinite articles (e.g., *a, an*)

Conjunctions (e.g., *and, than*)

Some forms of the verb *to be* (e.g., *are*)

When the vowel sound is reduced, it becomes a schwa (ə), or may almost disappear ('). A schwa sounds like *uh*.

🎧 1.14 Listen to the first part of segment 1 of the student presentation. Notice the reduced vowels:

> *"The Maldives 'r in the beautiful warm waters 'v the Indian Ocean. It looks like ə nice place t' visit, doesn't it? ə lot 'v people think so. More th'n ə million tourists visit the Maldives every year."*

K **🎧 1.14** Work with a partner. Listen and practice saying the reduced vowels in the excerpt below.

> *"The Maldives 'r in the beautiful warm waters 'v the Indian Ocean. It looks like ə nice place t' visit, doesn't it? ə lot 'v people think so. More th'n ə million tourists visit the Maldives every year."*

L **🎧 1.15** Work with a partner. Read the excerpt from segment 1 of the presentation. Underline the words you think have reduced vowels. Then listen and check your work as a class.

> *"In our class we've talked a lot about climate change. But many people are getting kind of tired of the topic. Why don't we take it more seriously? Maybe because most of the impact of climate change is in the future, it's easy not to think about the effects. But to the people of the Maldives, the effects are already very real."*

M Work with a partner. Student A says the excerpt from exercise L while Student B listens. Student B checks [✓] each vowel Student A correctly reduces. Then change roles.

How I swam the North Pole

" Climate change is for real, and we need to do something about it . . . right now. **"**

BEFORE YOU WATCH

A Work with a small group. Read the information about the TED speaker. Then answer the questions.

1. *Sustainable* means able to continue for a long time. What do you think Pugh means by *a sustainable world*?

2. How do you think Pugh's swim might bring attention to the issue of climate change?

LEWIS PUGH   Coldwater Swimmer

Lewis Pugh is considered the greatest coldwater swimmer in history. However, he doesn't swim to win races. Instead, he swims to draw the world's attention to environmental issues. Pugh believes that we all need to make changes in our lives in order to slow climate change. He asks, "What decisions are we going to make today to ensure that we all live in a sustainable world?"

Lewis Pugh's idea worth spreading is that sometimes we have to do extraordinary things in order to call attention to important issues.

B COLLABORATE Work with a small group. What do you know about the North Pole? Read the following statements and write T for *true* or F for *false*. Then explain your answers to other members of your group.

> A: *I think the North Pole is frozen all year, right?*
> B: *I think so, too.*

1. _____ It is frozen all year long.

2. _____ It is the coldest place on earth.

3. _____ Now it has less ice than 100 years ago.

4. _____ It is covered by sea water and sea ice.

5. _____ It is in Antarctica.

VOCABULARY

C 🎧 **1.16** The sentences below will help you learn words in the TED Talk. Read and listen to the sentences. Guess the meaning of each bold word. Then match each word to the correct definition on page 34.

a. He **gasped** for air because the cold temperature made it difficult to breathe.

b. Air and water **expand** when they get hotter.

c. After months of training, he was **mentally** exhausted and could not think anymore.

d. Everyone was very **emotional** when they saw that the orphaned polar bear cubs had died. Some people were crying.

e. The Arctic is one of the coldest **regions** on Earth.

f. The beauty of the ice **drew** many tourists to the Arctic last year.

g. After a few minutes in Arctic **conditions**, your hands and feet become numb. You can't feel anything.

h. The sea is likely to rise more than 200 feet. Just to **put** that **in perspective,** 200 feet is about the height of a 20-story building.

i. As the climate gets warmer, the glaciers begin to **retreat.** The Columbia Glacier in Alaska has shrunk by over nine miles in the last 25 years.

j. The balloon became larger and larger until finally, it **burst.**

1. _____ (n) geographic areas

2. _____ (v) attracted

3. _____ (v) broke open as a result of pressure

4. _____ (n) the situation in which people live or work

5. _____ (v) breathed in quickly

6. _____ (adv) in a manner that is related to the mind or thinking

7. _____ (v) move back

8. _____ (v) increase in size

9. _____ (v) give some context

10. _____ (adj) full of strong feeling

D COMMUNICATE Work with a partner. Discuss the statements and questions below. Use the words in bold in your answers.

1. Describe activities that you find **mentally** challenging.

2. Describe a favorite **region** of your country.

3. Describe an **emotional** event in your life.

4. Describe an activity, event, or issue that you have spent a lot of time on. What **drew** you to it?

5. Describe the worst weather **conditions** you have ever seen.

Polar bear on Arctic sea ice

WATCH

E ▶ **1.6** **WATCH FOR MAIN IDEAS** Watch the edited TED Talk by Lewis Pugh. Check [✓] the most important idea that Pugh wants his audience to take away.

1. ☐ Swimming can be a symbolic act.

2. ☐ The Arctic is a very beautiful place.

3. ☐ The North Pole is changing because of melting sea ice.

4. ☐ Climate change needs to be addressed by everyone immediately.

F ▶ **1.6** **WATCH FOR DETAILS** Watch the edited TED Talk again. Choose the best answer to complete each statement.

1. Pugh visited the Arctic for the first time _____.

    a. when he was a child   **b.** seven years before his swim   **c.** just before his swim

2. Pugh says that about _____ of the Arctic sea ice has melted away.

    a. ten percent   **b.** a quarter   **c.** half

3. The temperature of the water at the North Pole is _____.

    a. below freezing   **b.** above freezing   **c.** at the freezing point

4. When Pugh did his test swim, _____.

    a. his fingers froze   **b.** his goggles froze   **c.** he stopped breathing

5. Pugh's swim across the North Pole lasted about _____.

    a. ten minutes   **b.** twenty minutes   **c.** forty-five minutes

learnmore The *Titanic* was the world's biggest passenger ship when it was built in 1911. On its first voyage across the North Atlantic ocean, it crashed into an iceberg and sank. Over 1,500 people died in the icy waters off of Newfoundland, Canada.

WORDS IN THE TALK

become extinct (v): no longer exist
cells (n): basic units in living things
glacier (n): a huge block of ice that moves slowly over land
swollen (adj): enlarged; bigger
wobble (n): an unsteadiness, lack of balance

NOTE-TAKING SKILL Use Short Phrases

When you take notes, write important words and short phrases. Don't write full sentences. This will help you take notes quickly and remember more after you listen.

Full Sentence:

The Maldives built a sea wall around the main island of Male.

In the meeting, Maldivian leaders signed a document pleading with world leaders to work together against climate change.

Short Phrases:

Built sea wall—Male

Document—stop climate change

(See page 169 in the *Independent Student Handbook* for more information on using short phrases in notes.)

G ▶ **1.7** Watch Segments 1 and 2 of the edited TED Talk. As you watch, complete the sentences with words you hear.

Segment 1

1. Ever since I think I was just six years old, I dreamed of going to the polar regions. I really, really wanted to go to the _____.

2. But I have seen that place _____ beyond all description, just in that short period of time.

3. I have seen polar bears walking across very, very _____ ice in search of food.

4. And I have also, every year, seen _____ sea ice. And I wanted the world to know what was happening up there.

5. In the two years before my swim, 23 percent of the arctic sea ice cover just _____ away.

6. _____ change is for real, and we need to do something about it.

Segment 2

7. And on day four, we decided to just do a quick _____ test swim.

8. I have never in my life felt anything like that moment. I could barely _____. I was gasping for air. I was hyperventilating so much, and within seconds my hands were _____.

9. And I remember taking the goggles off my face and looking down at my hands in sheer shock, because my _____ had swollen so much that they were like sausages.

H Rewrite the nine sentences from exercise G in note form. Use short phrases.

1. _____

2. _____

3. _____

4. _____

5. _____

6. _____

7. _____

8. _____

9. _____

Pugh's Arctic Swim

Distance: **1 km (0.62 miles)**
Time: **18m 50s**
Temperature: **29F (−2C)**

Lewis Pugh swimming into the icy waters
of the North Pole

I ▶ **1.8** **EXPAND YOUR VOCABULARY** Watch the excerpts from the TED Talk. Guess the meanings of the words and phrases in the box.

> come true   beyond all description   hitched a ride   in shock   in agony

J **WATCH MORE** Go to TED.com to watch the full TED Talk by Lewis Pugh.

AFTER YOU WATCH

K **THINK CRITICALLY** **Reflect.** Work in a small group and answer these questions.

1. What effect did Pugh's swim have on him?
2. How do you think Pugh's swim will impact people's views on climate change?

L **THINK CRITICALLY** **Evaluate.** Work with a small group. Discuss your answers to the questions below.

1. Pugh says it was a *"symbolic"* swim. How do you think it was symbolic?
2. What does Pugh mean when he says he wanted to *"shake the lapels"* of world leaders about climate change? Do you think it was a good strategy? Explain your answer.

Male narwhals gather to eat at Lancaster Sound in Canada.

Put It Together

A THINK CRITICALLY Synthesize. Work with a small group. Check [✓] which strategies each speaker uses to persuade his or her audience that the loss of polar ice is important. Then discuss what each speaker actually said.

> A: *The student presenter gives examples of what could happen in the future.*
>
> B: *Right. She said that the sea level would rise.*

STRATEGY	PART 1 STUDENT PRESENTATION	PART 2 TED TALK
Tells a personal story		
Gives examples of what could happen in the future		
Provides evidence of current impact of climate change		

COMMUNICATE

ASSIGNMENT: Individual Presentation You are going to give an individual presentation about an environmental or social topic that is important to you. Review the ideas in Parts 1 and 2 and the listening and speaking skills as you prepare your presentation.

PREPARE

PRESENTATION SKILL **Make an Emotional Connection**

When you present, you should try to connect the audience emotionally to your topic. This will help persuade the audience of your point of view. Here are some ways to create an emotional connection to the audience:

1. Present information that gets a reaction. The information might make the audience surprised, curious, or worried. It could also make the audience question their assumptions. For example, in Part 1, the student speaker used maps to show what might happen if all Earth's sea ice melted.

2. Share a moving personal story. Make sure your words show your feelings about the event or time that you're describing. For example, in Part 2, Lewis Pugh spoke about his painful swim in the North Pole.

B Work in a small group. What environmental or social issue are you most interested in? Add your ideas to the list below.

- Lack of access to clean water

- World hunger

- Lack of access to education for girls

- Too much garbage or waste

- _____

- _____

C Choose one of the issues from exercise B for your presentation. Answer the questions below.

Issue

1. What issue are you going to present?

_____

2. Why should people take this issue seriously?

_____

3. What ideas have you heard about that try to address this issue?

_____

_____

Causes and Effects

4. What are the causes of the problem you have chosen?

_____

_____

5. What are some of the effects?

_____

_____

6. What words will you use to describe these causes and effects?

_____

Make an Emotional Connection

7. How will you make an emotional connection with your audience? Use one of the ideas from the Presentation Skill box on page 39.

_____

D Work with a partner. Practice your presentation. Ask your partner if your presentation was persuasive.

E Read the rubric on page 179 before you present. Notice how your presentation will be evaluated. Keep these categories in mind as you present and watch your classmates' presentations.

PRESENT

F Give your presentation to the class. Watch your classmates' presentations. After you watch each one, provide feedback using the rubric as a guide. Add notes or any other feedback you want to share.

G **THINK CRITICALLY** **Evaluate.** In your group, discuss the feedback you received. As a class, discuss what each group did well and what might make each presentation even stronger.

REFLECT

Reflect on what you have learned. Check [✓] your progress.

I can
- ☐ listen for details.
- ☐ talk about causes and effects.
- ☐ reduce vowels.
- ☐ use short phrases in notes.
- ☐ make an emotional connection with the audience.

I understand the meanings of these words and can use them.
Circle those you know. Underline those you need to work on.

artificial	current	expand AWL	put in perspective AWL
barely	document AWL	gasp	region AWL
burst	dramatic AWL	mentally AWL	retreat
condition	draw	predict AWL	symbolic AWL
consequence AWL	emotional	protection	take seriously

UNIT 3
Unexpected Discoveries

A tourist looks out of a window of a house designed by the famous architect Antoni Gaudí in Barcelona, Spain.

THINK AND DISCUSS

1 Read the unit title. Look at the photo and read the caption. How do you think the photo relates to the title?

2 What are some things that people discover? How do they make these kinds of discoveries?

43

BEFORE YOU LISTEN

A COMMUNICATE Work with a partner. Discuss these questions.

1. What do you know about the invention of objects that you use every day?

2. Look at the photo and read the caption. What skills or qualities do you think an inventor and this artist might have in common?

A sculpture made entirely of paper clips by the artist Pietro D'Angelo

VOCABULARY

B 🎧 **1.17** Read and listen to the sentences with words from the podcast you will hear. Guess the meanings of the words in bold. Then choose the correct meaning.

1. Many people did not understand the **significance** of the discovery, but Spencer realized that it could lead to big changes in our lives.

   Significance means:

   a. convenience   **b.** importance   **c.** quality

2. Some people have a **talent** for understanding mechanical things. They enjoy fixing cars and other machines.

   Talent means:

   a. qualification   **b.** inspiration   **c.** natural ability

3. When I have to really concentrate on my work, I **tune out** everything else that is going on around me.

   Tune out means:

   a. listen to   **b.** reduce   **c.** ignore

4. The noisy students in the library were **annoying,** but I was able to finish my assignment anyway.

   Annoying means:

   a. causing great anger

   b. causing some frustration

   c. gradually increasing

5. There are many **potential** uses for this new technology, but it will take time to develop it.

   Potential means:

   a. possible   **b.** separate   **c.** immediate

6. Engineers are **capable of** looking at a problem from several different perspectives.

   To be **capable of** something means:

   a. to be prepared

   b. to be more likely

   c. to have the power or skill

7. The project took a long time, but we **eventually** finished it.

   Eventually means:

   a. probably

   b. with great difficulty

   c. in the end

8. The **theme** for this year's conference is "Discoveries in the New Century."

Theme means:

a. main topic   **b.** news   **c.** best idea

9. We need to **focus on** this task for now. We can't start thinking about the next one yet.

To **focus on** means:

a. to work hard   **b.** to direct attention to   **c.** to keep up with

10. The work of many different scientists contributed to this invention. **In a way,** it was a team effort, not the work of a single inventor.

In a way means:

a. it is partly true that

b. it is most likely that

c. it cannot be said that

C COMMUNICATE Work with a partner. Discuss these questions. Use the words in bold in your answers.

A: *To focus on my homework, I go to the library.*
B: *Yes, it's nice and quiet there.*

1. What do you do when you really want to **focus on** something?

2. How do you to **tune out** noise when you are studying?

3. What is something you find **annoying?**

4. What are some of your special or unusual **talents?** Explain them to your partner.

Inventor Percy Spencer with the microwave he invented

D **THINK CRITICALLY** Predict. Work with a partner. Look at the photo and read the caption. You are going to listen to a podcast on the topic of serendipity. Serendipity is when something good happens by chance. Discuss these questions.

1. What do you think serendipity has to do with Percy Spencer and the microwave oven?

2. Do you think inventors like Percy Spencer think differently than other people?

LISTEN

E 🎧 **1.18** **LISTEN FOR MAIN IDEAS** Listen to the podcast. Check [✓] three statements that you think the hosts of the podcast would agree with.

1. ☐ Some inventors have different ways of thinking.

2. ☐ Serendipity is mostly good luck.

3. ☐ Inventions are about 90 percent accidental.

4. ☐ Serendipity is probably only a small part of the process of invention.

5. ☐ Anyone can learn to think more creatively.

F 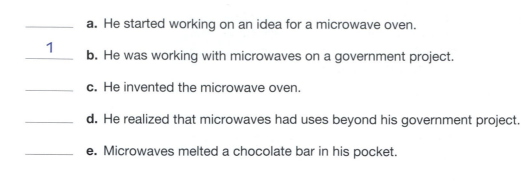 **1.19 LISTEN FOR DETAILS** Listen to segment 1 of the podcast. Put the events of Spencer's life in the correct order from 1 to 5.

_____ **a.** He started working on an idea for a microwave oven.

__1__ **b.** He was working with microwaves on a government project.

_____ **c.** He invented the microwave oven.

_____ **d.** He realized that microwaves had uses beyond his government project.

_____ **e.** Microwaves melted a chocolate bar in his pocket.

G **1.20 LISTEN FOR DETAILS** Listen to segment 2 of the podcast. Complete the mind map with the information below. Write the correct phrase in each cell.

a. divergent thinking
b. connections between ideas
c. the beginning of ideas

d. things they were not looking for
e. potential solutions

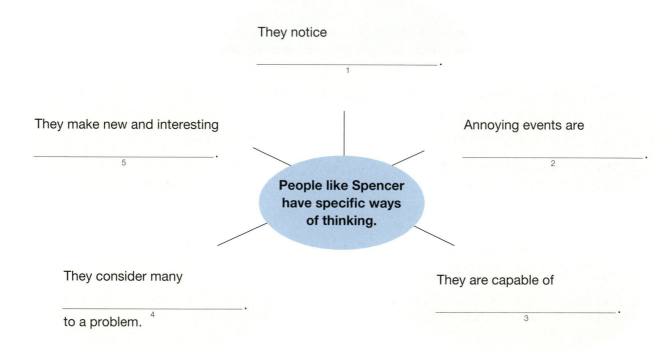

They notice

_____1_____ .

They make new and interesting

_____5_____ .

People like Spencer have specific ways of thinking.

Annoying events are

_____2_____ .

They consider many

_____ .
to a problem. 4

They are capable of

_____3_____ .

When you listen, you can often make inferences or infer meaning from what you hear. You can guess what the speaker means even if he or she does not say it directly. Good listeners combine information from different sources to make inferences. This information may include the following:

1. What the speaker says and how he or she says it:

   "I won't use a microwave oven!"

   Listeners can infer that the speaker thinks there is something bad about microwave ovens, perhaps that they are dangerous or ineffective.

2. What they already know about the topic:

   "Spencer's story shows the difference between the terms 'discovery' and 'invention.' First, came the melted chocolate bar. Then came the microwave."

   Listeners can infer the meanings of the terms *discovery* and *invention* by their understanding of the events: first, a melted chocolate bar (discovery), and then a microwave (invention).

H **1.21** **INFER MEANING** Work with a partner. Listen again to excerpts from the conversation. Check [✓] the inference you can make from what the speaker says.

1. *"He realized that the microwaves had done it. That made him think—wow— maybe microwaves could be useful, not just for his government project but for something else."*

   a. ☐ Spencer realized he was going to make a lot of money.

   b. ☐ Spencer thought microwaves would be useful in cooking.

   c. ☐ Spencer decided to leave the project and work on ovens instead.

2. *"Some people call it serendipity, but it turns out that it's a bit more than just good luck … First, they notice things that they were not looking for. A lot of us focus so much on our goals that we tune out everything else."*

   a. ☐ Spencer knew the value of serendipity.

   b. ☐ Divergent thinkers are often unsuccessful.

   c. ☐ We lose opportunities when we focus too much on goals.

3. *"Yes, some people are more likely to notice things and make interesting and new connections between ideas. They recognize opportunities. In a way, they create serendipity."*

   a. ☐ It is important to recognize these opportunities when they arise.

   b. ☐ Serendipity is all in the imagination.

   c. ☐ We are not all equally likely to experience serendipity.

AFTER YOU LISTEN

▍ **COMMUNICATE** Look at the graphic below. Then answer these questions with a partner.

1. What happens as we get older, according to the graphic? What might be the reason for this change?

2. What might be the consequences of this change, especially for invention and discovery?

3. Do you think there is a way to increase the percentage of adults who are capable of divergent thinking? Explain your answer.

Who is capable of divergent thinking?

4–5 year olds 98%

8–10 year olds 32%

13–15 year olds 10%

Adults 2%

As divergent thinkers, children see many possible uses for objects.

SPEAKING

SPEAKING SKILL Check Your Understanding

There are many ways to check—and get a better understanding of—what someone has just said.

1. If you heard but did not understand the meaning of a word, repeat it with rising intonation:

> A: *Some inventions happened because of a lucky break.*
>
> B: *Lucky break?*

2. If you didn't understand part of what the speaker said, repeat the part that you *did* understand.

> A: *I think he's a divergent thinker.*
>
> B: *You think he's a what?*

3. To confirm your understanding, use the phrases below:

> *So, are you saying that _____? / So, what you mean is _____?*

4. To clarify what a speaker said, use the following phrases:

> *What do you mean?*
>
> *How's that? / How so?*
>
> *I am not sure I understand. / I am not sure I follow.*

J 🎧 **1.22** Read the excerpts from the podcast. Then listen and complete how the host checked for understanding.

Host: And welcome back to *Conversations*. Today's theme—chance.

Co-host: Actually, the show is really about serendipity.

Host: _____₁_____?

Co-host: Right, serendipity.

Co-host: Was this a case of serendipity? Partly, but I think it was also Spencer.

Host: Really? _____₂_____?

Co-host: Well, other people had noticed that microwaves could melt things, but Spencer was the one who understood its significance.

Host: What _____₃_____ thinking?

Co-host: *Divergent.* Divergent thinkers consider many potential solutions to a problem.

Host: Hmm. _____₄_____ I follow.

Can you give us _____₅_____?

Co-host: Sure.

PART 1   51

Co-host: But a divergent thinker might see lots of other possible functions; for example, to mark a place in a book, or you could unfold it and use it to punch a hole in something.

Host: I see. _____ some people have a special talent for
this? It's not serendipity at all?

Co-host: Yes, some people are more likely to notice things and make interesting and new connections between ideas.

PRONUNCIATION SKILL *Can* and *Can't*

Can and *can't* are both spelled with *c-a-n*, but their pronunciation is often different when they come before a verb in a statement or question.

🎧 **1.23**

Pronounce *can* with a reduced vowel /ə/. It sounds as if there is almost no vowel at all:

> *I /kn/ speak English pretty well.*

Always pronounce *can't* with a full vowel sound:

> *I /kænt/ speak Arabic at all.*

K 🎧 **1.24** Listen to the following excerpts and choose *can* or *can't*.

1. *"What was special about Spencer? This **can** / **can't** be the only example of this. I wondered how often this happens."*

2. *"Hmm. I am not sure I follow. **Can** / **Can't** you give us an example?"*

3. *"So, why **can't** / **can** I do this? **Can** / **Can't** we learn to be better at this kind of thinking?"*

4. *"Absolutely, there are lots of exercises you **can** / **can't** do to help you notice things and think more creatively. The paperclip example is a good place to start. Try to think of as many new uses as you **can** / **can't**."*

5. *"We **can** / **can't** actually increase the possibility of serendipity by changing the way we think?"*

L Work with a partner. Take turns repeating the excerpts from exercise K with the correct pronunciation of *can* and *can't*.

M **THINK CRITICALLY** Apply. Are you a divergent thinker? Work with a partner. Follow the steps below. Use confirmation and clarification checks to make sure you understand what your partner says. Use correct pronunciation for *can* and *can't*.

SPHERE	HALF SPHERE	CUBE	CONE	CYLINDER
WIRE	TUBE	FLAT SQUARE	BRACKET	RECTANGULAR BLOCK
HOOK	PAIR OF WHEELS	CROSS	RING	HANDLE

1. Choose three of these shapes.

2. Put the shapes together in different ways. Create new objects that could be used in the following ways:

   a. as a piece of furniture

   b. as a tool

   c. as a toy

   d. as a personal item (e.g., a comb, a bookmark, etc.)

3. Draw your new inventions on a piece of paper and share with the class.

N **THINK CRITICALLY** Reflect. Work with a partner. Do you think activities like this can change the way you think? Explain your answer.

A: *This activity really makes me think in new ways.*

B: *Right! You have to think differently to do it.*

Happy maps

❝ [A] journey to work became one thing only: the shortest path. **❞**

BEFORE YOU WATCH

A Work with a small group. Read the title of the talk and the information about the TED speaker. Then discuss these questions.

1. Do you use maps? When do you use them?

2. What do you think a "happy map" is?

DANIELE QUERCIA Map Researcher

Daniele Quercia is interested in how people interact with their environment, both online and in the real world. He uses social media and large amounts of data to understand this relationship. Quercia wants to use this information to make our lives happier and more satisfying.

Quercia's idea worth spreading is that the fastest route may be efficient, but not always enjoyable. There are times when taking a different route can be more memorable and joyful.

VOCABULARY

B 🎧 **1.25** The sentences below will help you learn words in the TED Talk. Read and listen to the sentences. Guess the meanings of the words in bold. Then match each word to its definition.

a. People often feel a sense of **shame** after they have done something stupid or wrong.

b. My **commute** to work usually takes an hour—even longer if there is a lot of traffic.

c. The road is closed for repair so we have to take a **detour**.

d. An effective team listens to everyone's idea and then tries to come to a **consensus**.

e. Map apps on smartphones were real **game changers**. Not many people use paper maps anymore.

f. There is not enough data to make a **definitive** conclusion, but we can make a very good guess.

g. I could not **recall** the location of the office, so I used my map app.

h. Following a big snowstorm, some motorists were **trapped** in their cars for hours.

i. We interviewed a lot of people about the traffic problems, and slowly, a solution began to **emerge**.

j. Always taking the quickest route may **rob** you **of** the chance to see the beautiful countryside.

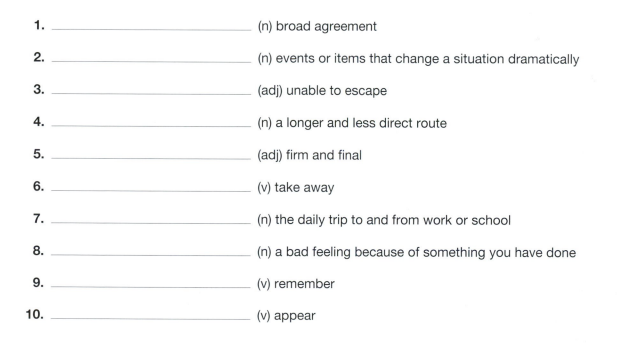

1. _____ (n) broad agreement

2. _____ (n) events or items that change a situation dramatically

3. _____ (adj) unable to escape

4. _____ (n) a longer and less direct route

5. _____ (adj) firm and final

6. _____ (v) take away

7. _____ (n) the daily trip to and from work or school

8. _____ (n) a bad feeling because of something you have done

9. _____ (v) remember

10. _____ (v) appear

C **COMMUNICATE** Work with a partner. Discuss these questions. Use the items in bold in your answers.

> A: *My **commute** is about half an hour. What about yours?*
>
> B: *You're lucky. Mine is over an hour.*

1. How long is your **commute** to work or school?

2. Do you use a mobile app that shows you one **definitive** route to your destination?

3. If so, do you ever choose a different route—a **detour?** Why, or why not?

4. How can you help a group of people reach a **consensus?**

WATCH

D ▶ **1.9** **WATCH FOR MAIN IDEAS** Watch the edited TED Talk. Check [✓] the statement that best expresses the speaker's main idea.

1. ☐ Collecting personal data can improve maps.

2. ☐ Mobile mapping apps are likely to improve in the future.

3. ☐ The happy path is better than the most direct one.

4. ☐ You can make surprising discoveries by taking a different path.

5. ☐ The route from A to B is filled with emotion.

---

learnmore Mass Ave (short for Massachusetts Avenue) is a street that connects Boston to Cambridge, two neighboring cities in Massachusetts. Stores, apartments, and restaurants line the 16-mile street. In addition, many subway stations, bus stops, and crowded sidewalks make Mass Ave one of the busiest roads in the city.

WORDS IN THE TALK

aesthetics (n): sense of beauty
aggregate (v): combine; put together
cartography (n): map making
crowdsourcing (n): getting support or ideas from a large number of people over the Internet
data mining (n): computer analysis of large amounts of data to find patterns
PhD (n): the highest academic degree

NOTE-TAKING SKILL Make a Time Line

Often speakers use chronological (time) order when they describe an event. In other words, they explain what happened first, second, next, and so on. You can use this time order to help organize your notes. Listen for the following references to times and dates:

in + year, on + day, by

since, ago, when, for

during, before, after

now, then, next, later

You can create a picture of events using a time line. For example:

| Graduated college | Got 1st job | After 2 years, got promoted | Made vice president |

E ▶ **1.10** **WATCH FOR DETAILS** Watch segment 1 of Quercia's edited TED Talk. Listen for the signals of time order below. Check each one as you hear it. Then complete the time line with the correct information. Watch the segment again to check your answers.

_____ *A few years ago …*	_____ *… one day*
_____ *. . . after …*	_____ *After a feeling of …*
_____ *After a month …*	_____ *After that experience …*

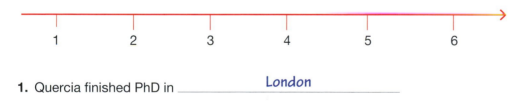

1   2   3   4   5   6

1. Quercia finished PhD in _____ London _____

2. Moved to _____

3. Cycled to _____ every day

4. One day took _____

5. Felt surprised, then felt _____

6. Changed focus of his _____

F ▶ **1.11** **WATCH FOR DETAILS** Complete the summary of segment 2 of the edited TED Talk. Then watch the segment to check your answers.

Quercia and his colleagues built a crowd-sourcing platform, a

_____ . Thousands of players looked at two city
                    1

scenes. They had to choose the scene that they thought was more beautiful, quiet,

and _____ . Based on the players' answers, they
                    2

are able to see which are the urban _____ that
                                              3

make people happy. In tests, participants found the happy, the beautiful, the quiet

path far more _____ than the shortest one, and
                        4

just by adding a few minutes to _____ time.
                                              5

G ▶ **1.12** **EXPAND YOUR VOCABULARY** Watch the excerpts from the TED Talk. Guess the meanings of the words and phrases in the box.

> as opposed to   looking people in the eyes   don't get me wrong   team up with

H **WATCH MORE** Go to TED.com to watch the full TED Talk by Daniele Quercia.

AFTER YOU WATCH

I **THINK CRITICALLY** **Infer.** Work with a partner. Read the excerpts from Quercia's talk. Choose the best inference from the statement in bold.

1. *"In this single journey, there was no thought of enjoying the road, no pleasure in connecting with nature, no possibility of looking people in the eyes. And why? **Because I was saving a minute out of my commute.**"*

 a. The commute was not very pleasant, so a shorter commute was better.

 b. Saving the minute was not as important as he thought.

 c. He was surprised that he had saved only a minute.

2. *"After that experience, I changed. **I changed my research from traditional data-mining to understanding how people experience the city.**"*

 a. Quercia's data-mining approach was not a good way to find out about people's emotions.

 b. He felt that his earlier work was very old-fashioned and he wanted to do something new.

 c. He didn't want to work with maps anymore. He wanted to build more games.

3. *"In tests, participants found the happy, the beautiful, the quiet path far more enjoyable than the shortest one, and just by adding a few minutes to travel time."*

  a. The ideas are still in the early stages. Quercia is still testing them.

  b. People will probably feel the same way in real-life conditions.

  c. People will start taking the happy and beautiful path.

J COMMUNICATE Discuss these questions in a small group. Then check your understanding of your classmates' answers by using confirmation and clarification questions.

1. Look at the map of London and read the captions. Based on the information, which route would you like to take? Why?

2. Would you take a more beautiful, happier, or quieter route to work or school? Why, or why not?

Start 🚆

End 🏛

Fast Route   2.5 miles
Taking 46 minutes, this route goes through very busy streets including The Strand.

Happy Route   2.8 miles
Taking 53 minutes, this route goes through quieter streets including historic Fleet Street.

Put It Together

A **THINK CRITICALLY** **Synthesize.** Work with a partner. Quercia quotes Albert Einstein, "Logic will get you from A to B. Imagination will take you everywhere." Discuss the questions.

1. What do you think Einstein's quote means?

2. How does this idea apply to Quercia's happy maps? What did logic do for him and his work? What did imagination do?

3. How could Einstein's ideas apply to Spencer's work on the microwave? What did logic do for him and his work? What did imagination do?

COMMUNICATE

ASSIGNMENT: **Individual Presentation** You are going to create and present your own happy map. Review the ideas in Parts 1 and 2 and the listening and speaking skills as you prepare your presentation.

PREPARE

PRESENTATION SKILL Pause

Speaking slowly and clearly during a presentation makes it easier for an audience to understand your ideas. Using pauses gives listeners more time to process and reflect on what they hear.

Listen to how Daniele Quercia pauses briefly but frequently in the following excerpt:

▶ **1.13** *"Imagination will take you everywhere.* [Pause] *So with a bit of imagination,* [Pause] *we needed to understand* [Pause] *which parts of the city* [Pause] *people find beautiful."*

B ▶ **1.14** Work with a partner. Watch this excerpt from Quercia's talk and mark (/) where you hear pauses. Then take turns saying it aloud. Check if your partner is pausing frequently enough.

"In tests, participants found the happy, the beautiful, the quiet path far more enjoyable than the shortest one, and that just by adding a few minutes to travel time. Participants also love to attach memories to places. Shared memories—that's where the old BBC building was; and personal memories—that's where I gave my first kiss."

C Prepare for your presentation.

- Make a map of your commute or another route that you often take.
- Try out a different route, one that is more beautiful, peaceful, or exciting.
- Make a map of your new, happy route.
- Make some notes about why the new route is a happy one.
  - o Describe the scene and things you see along the way.
  - o Think about your emotional response to the route.
  - o Compare it to your usual route.
- Include pictures if you can.

D Practice your presentation. Remember to pause and speak slowly but naturally.

E Read the rubric on page 180 before you present. Notice how your presentation will be evaluated. Keep these categories in mind as you present and watch your classmates' presentations.

PRESENT

F Give your presentation to the class. Watch your classmates' presentations. After you watch each one, provide feedback using the rubric as a guide. Add notes or any other feedback you want to share.

G **THINK CRITICALLY** **Evaluate.** In your group, discuss the feedback you received. As a class, discuss what each presenter did well and what might make each presentation even stronger.

REFLECT

Reflect on what you have learned. Check [✓] your progress.

I can
- ☐ infer meaning.
- ☐ check my understanding.
- ☐ pronounce *can* and *can't*.
- ☐ take notes using a time line.
- ☐ pause effectively.

I understand the meanings of these words and can use them.
Circle those you know. Underline those you need to work on.

annoying	detour	in a way	significance AWL
capable of AWL	emerge AWL	potential AWL	talent
commute	eventually AWL	recall	theme AWL
consensus AWL	focus on AWL	rob of something	trapped
definitive AWL	game changer	shame	tune out

The Business of Style

Fashion students Kiki McKenzie and Heather Dooley getting ready to show their latest designs

THINK AND DISCUSS

1 Read the title of the unit. What do you think this unit will be about?

2 Look at the photo. What do you think the advantages are of making your own clothes?

PART 1
Sneakerheads

Listening
Make Predictions

Speaking
Make Suggestions

Pronunciation
Numbers

PART 2
TEDTALKS

Danit Peleg
Forget shopping. Soon you'll download your new clothes.

Note Taking
Review Your Notes

PUT IT TOGETHER

Communicate
Interview a Partner

Presentation Skill
Prepare for an Interview

BEFORE YOU LISTEN

A COMMUNICATE Work with a partner. Look at the photo and read the caption. Discuss these questions.

1. Do you own a pair of sneakers? When do you wear them?

2. What factors are important to you when you buy sneakers? Do you have a favorite brand (such as Nike, Adidas, or Puma)?

3. Why do you think Cesar Vasquez owns 300 pairs of sneakers?

Cesar Vasquez, a sneakerhead in Los Angeles, owns 300 pairs of limited edition sneakers.

Listening to someone talk about unfamiliar content can be challenging. Making predictions about what you are going to hear is one way to make the content easier to understand.

To make predictions, think about the answers to these questions:

- What will you be listening to? Is it a lecture, a conversation, or an interview?
- Will there be more than one speaker? What do you know about the speaker(s)?
- Does the lecture or presentation have a title? If so, what do you know about the topic?

B MAKE PREDICTIONS Work with a partner. You are going to listen to a conversation among three students. They are planning a presentation about the sneaker business. Discuss these questions.

> A: *What do you think a sneakerhead is?*
>
> B: *Maybe a person who knows a lot about sneakers.*

1. Look at the photo on page 64. The title of Part 1 is "Sneakerheads." What do you think a sneakerhead is?

2. What do you think sneakerheads have to do with the sneaker business?

3. What aspects of the sneaker business do you think the students will talk about?

VOCABULARY

C 🎧 **1.26** Work with a partner. Read and listen to the sentences with words from the student conversation. Guess the meanings of the words in bold. Then match each word to its definition on page 66.

a. The **market** for sportswear, such as sneakers and exercise clothing, is very strong this year. More people are buying sportswear than last year.

b. There is a limited **supply** of these sneakers. Because of this, most people will have to wait months before they can buy them.

c. As more people keep fit, there is greater **demand** for sports clothing.

d. A white t-shirt is a **classic** example of clothing that always seems to be in style.

e. The **dominant** view among experts is that the business will be successful. However, a few experts believe that it will fail.

f. The strong sales of sneakers this year **demonstrate** their continuing popularity.

g. The company **releases** new styles every year, but the exact dates are always a surprise.

h. The **primary** customers for sportswear are people who play sports. However, other people buy these clothes as fashion accessories.

i. There was a **profile** of the company president in the newspaper. It had information about her background and her business philosophy.

j. The high quality and low price of these sneakers explain their **widespread** popularity. Everyone seems to be wearing them.

1. _dominant_ (adj) the most important; having the greatest influence

2. _____ (n) all the business related to a particular product

3. _____ (n) the amount of something that is available

4. _____ (adj) typical

5. _____ (adj) happening or existing in many places

6. _____ (v) makes available to the public

7. _____ (n) need

8. _____ (adj) first; main

9. _____ (n) description of a person's life and work

10. _____ (v) show

D COMMUNICATE Work with a partner. Take turns asking and answering the questions. Use the words in bold in your answers.

1. What happens when there is **demand** for a product, but the **supply** is limited?

2. How do companies **demonstrate** how their products work? Give examples.

3. What brands are **dominant** in the clothing **market** in your country?

4. What is a popular fashion style or item at the moment? Why do you think this popularity is so **widespread?**

5. Choose a product you know well. Who do you think is the **primary** customer for this product?

6. What, in your opinion, are some **classic** examples of products or fashions?

E Work with a partner. Discuss these questions.

A: *I now think sneakerheads are the primary customers for some sneakers.*
B: *Yes, the students are probably going to talk about the sneaker market.*

1. Have any of the predictions you made in exercise B on page 65 changed? Have your predictions changed because of the new words you have learned?

2. Can you make any new predictions?

LISTEN

F 🎧 **1.27** ▶ **1.15** **LISTEN FOR MAIN IDEAS** Read the statements below. Then listen to the conversation. Check [✓] two statements that best summarize what the students will include in their presentation.

In their presentation, the students will include

1. ☐ an explanation of supply and demand in the market.
2. ☐ a profile of the companies in the market.
3. ☐ a prediction about the future of the market.
4. ☐ a description of the secondary market.
5. ☐ an explanation of how to buy and sell high-end sneakers.

Shoppers wait outside a store in Germany to buy the new Nike Air Yeezy 2 sneaker.

G 🎧 **1.28 LISTEN FOR DETAILS** Listen to segment 1 of the student conversation. As you listen, complete the notes.

	PRIMARY MARKET	SECONDARY MARKET
THE HIGH-END SNEAKER MARKET		
Value of the market	_____ *$42 billion* _____ per year 1	_____ per year 3
How and where the market operates	People wait at stores for _____ to buy 2 new styles.	Sneakerheads buy most of these shoes _____ and pay 4 up to _____ the 5 original price.

H 🎧 **1.29 LISTEN FOR DETAILS** Listen to segment 2 of the student conversation. Choose the best word or phrase to complete each statement.

1. One reason that high-end sneakers are popular is their connection to ____*d*____.
   a. politicians
   b. young people
   c. movie stars
   d. athletes

2. One sneakerhead has over _____ pairs of sneakers.
   a. 300
   b. 2,000
   c. 3,000
   d. 30,000

3. A portfolio lists the _____ of stocks or other things that you own.
   a. profit
   b. location
   c. value
   d. sales

4. According to the quote the student mentions, your sneakers can show your _____.
   a. daily routine
   b. personality
   c. wealth
   d. age

AFTER YOU LISTEN

I **CONFIRM PREDICTIONS** Work with a partner. Review your predictions from exercise B on page 65. Discuss whether your predictions were correct.

J **THINK CRITICALLY** **Infer.** Work with a partner. Read the excerpts from the student conversation. Then discuss the questions.

1. One of the students says, "I'll bet a lot of people don't realize that sneakers are a 42-billion-dollar-a-year business." Why does he think this figure will surprise people?

2. One of the students quotes from a movie about sneakerheads: *"There are a handful of things that can define who you are without saying a word. And your shoes are one of them."* How can shoes define someone?

SPEAKING

K Work in a small group. Look at the photos of sneakers below and throughout Part 1 of this unit. Which ones do you like the most and why?

L 🎧 **1.30** Listen and match the words and phrases (a–f) to the suggestions (1–6). Then listen and check your answers.

a. I suggest we first explain

b. It would be a good idea to point out that

c. How about

d. We should

e. What about a

f. Let's talk about

1. ___*d*___ present the sneaker market as a great example of supply and demand.

2. _____ profile of a famous sneakerhead?

3. _____ this is only part of the picture.

4. _____ the secondary market, too.

5. _____ what the secondary market is.

6. _____ meeting around 9:15 or 9:30?

M Work with a small group. What other ideas could the students include in their presentation? How could they make their presentation more interesting? Make three suggestions for what they should say or do.

> A: *They should wear sneakers to the presentation!*

PRONUNCIATION SKILL Numbers

Pronouncing numbers is an important speaking skill. Errors in pronunciation can result in misunderstandings.

🎧 **1.31**

1. Pronounce numbers ending in *-teen* with a clear *t* sound and stress on the *teen* syllable.

   14: four**teen**

2. Pronounce numbers ending in *-ty* with a *d* sound in the *ty* syllable and stress on the first syllable.

   40: **forty**

3. Say numbers between 1,100 and 10,000* in two different ways:

   1,100

   one thousand, one hundred (more formal)

   eleven hundred (less formal; more common)

   * Numbers that are exact thousands (e.g., 2,000, 3,000) are pronounced only in the first, more formal way.

N 🎧 **1.32** Listen to the excerpts from the student conversation and write in the numbers you hear. Then say the number or numbers in each excerpt using the correct pronunciation.

1. "A lot of people don't realize that sneakers are a _____ -billion-dollar-a-year business."

2. "Nike controls more than _____ percent of the U.S. sneaker market."

3. "Profit margins are about _____ percent."

4. "I saw a pair of Air Jordans for sale online for almost $_____."

5. "How about meeting around _____ or _____ at my place to finish up?"

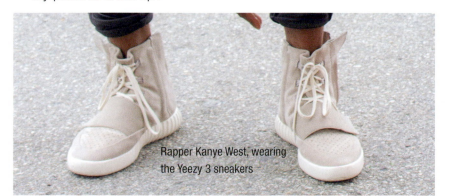
Rapper Kanye West, wearing the Yeezy 3 sneakers

THE SECONDARY MARKET FOR SNEAKERS

1 in 4 sneakers sold through online retailer eBay

-1%
LEBRON X LAVA

400%
ADIDAS
YEEZY BOOST

504%
KOBE
GRINCH

660%
AIR
FOAMPOSITE
ONE

1600%
AIR YEAZY
RED OCTOBER

2800%
DUNK SB
NYC PIGEON

95%
Nike market share

$1.2 bn
Value of Market

Change from original price for selected sneakers sold in secondary market

O THINK CRITICALLY **Interpret an Infographic.** Work with a small group. Study the infograph, and then discuss these questions.

1. Which two sneakers have shown the biggest change in price?

2. If you had a sneaker portfolio, which of these shoes would you *not* want in it?

3. How much would a pair of *Air Yeazy Red October* sneakers cost on the secondary market if the original price was $100? Who do you think would buy them?

4. Why do you think sneaker prices on the secondary market can be much higher than the original ones?

P THINK CRITICALLY **Reflect.** Many sneakerheads never wear the sneakers they buy. Does this surprise you? Why, or why not? Why do you think they buy them?

Forget shopping. Soon you'll download your new clothes.

❝ I wonder what our world will look like when our clothes will be digital. ❞

BEFORE YOU WATCH

A Work with a partner. Read the information about the TED speaker. Then discuss these questions.

1. What do you know about 3D printing?

2. Would you like to print your own clothes on a 3D printer? Why, or why not?

DANIT PELEG Fashion Designer

Danit Peleg is a fashion designer who also loves to experiment with new technology. She created one of the first 3D-printed fashion collections, producing all of the garments using only home printers.

Peleg's idea worth spreading is that technology can give designers more independence and can give the public greater access to all kinds of fashion.

B MAKE PREDICTIONS Work with a small group. Discuss these questions.

1. How could 3D printing make it easier for people to get fashionable clothes?

2. What topics do you think Peleg will talk about next?

VOCABULARY

C 🎧 **1.33** The sentences below will help you learn words in the TED Talk. Read and listen to the sentences. Guess the meaning of each bold word. Then choose the best meaning.

1. The 3D printer printed a shirt in separate pieces. She then **assembled** the pieces.

   Assemble means:

   a. put together   **b.** return   **c.** mail

2. My printer is making a really **weird** sound. I've never heard it make this noise before.

   Weird means:

   a. poor   **b.** strange   **c.** loud

3. 3D printing is a real **breakthrough** in the field. It will make a huge difference because it will allow custom work, that is, clothes designed especially for one person.

   A **breakthrough** is:

   a. an important development   **b.** a difficult situation   **c.** a useful strategy

4. This plastic is very **flexible** so you can change its shape and it will not break.

   Flexible means:

   a. very strong

   b. easy to see through

   c. easy to bend

5. In the past, only professionals designed new styles, but this new software has **empowered** ordinary people to design their own clothes.

   Empower means:

   a. allow

   b. supply

   c. require

6. We **modified** the design because the original one was too difficult to print.

   Modify means:

   a. reduce

   b. change

   c. recreate

7. I only have the older **version** of this software. The new one will not be released until next month.

A **version** is a:

a. form **b.** language **c.** code

8. The price of 3D printers has decreased **significantly** in the last couple of years.

Significantly means:

a. eventually **b.** a lot **c.** quickly

9. The pace of change has **accelerated** in recent years. It is difficult to keep up with everything that is happening.

Accelerate means:

a. become frustrating **b.** move faster **c.** develop differently

10. This technology will **evolve** and will continue to improve in the coming years.

Evolve means:

a. become more expensive **b.** increase **c.** develop gradually

D Work with a partner. Discuss these questions.

1. Have any of the predictions you made in exercise B on page 74 changed? Have your predictions changed because of the new words you have learned?

2. Can you make any new predictions? Discuss them with your partner.

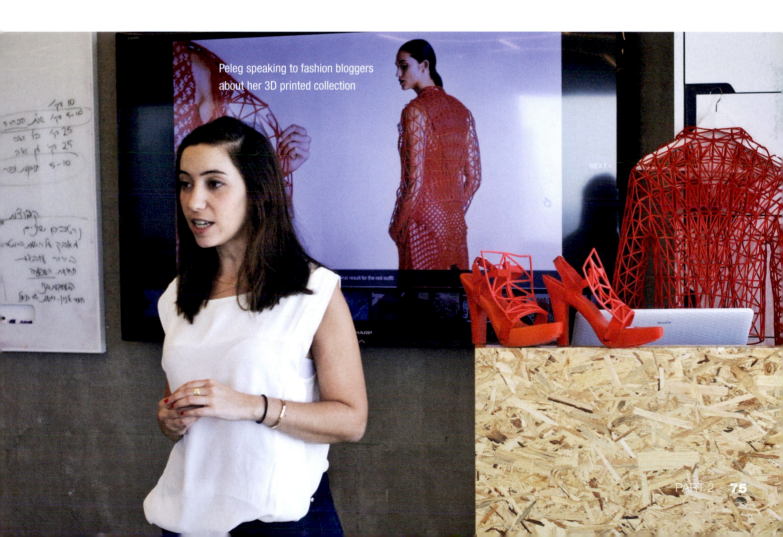

Peleg speaking to fashion bloggers about her 3D printed collection

E **COMMUNICATE** Work with a partner. Discuss these questions. Use the words in bold in your answers.

> A: *I think the biggest **breakthrough** has been in telecommunications.*
>
> B: *Yes, having a **smartphone** has **significantly** changed my life.*

1. What do you think have been the most important **breakthroughs** in technology in the past 50 years? Have they affected your life **significantly?** How?

2. Have new technologies **empowered** you to do anything new or different? Explain your answer.

3. In what ways do you think people's relationship with technology has **evolved?**

WATCH

F ▶ **1.16** **WATCH FOR DETAILS** Read the statements. Then watch segment 1 of Peleg's edited TED Talk. Write T for *true* or F for *false* for each statement.

1. _____ Peleg has a program on her computer that lets her design clothes.

2. _____ It took most of the night to print her skirt on a 3D printer.

3. _____ The skirt came out of the printer ready to wear.

NOTE-TAKING SKILL Review Your Notes

Taking notes is a process. It does not stop at the end of a lecture or a class. It is difficult to decide what is most important *while* you are listening. However, it is both useful and important to return to your notes *after* listening and review them to decide on the speaker's main ideas. Leave room at the bottom of the page to add the main ideas.

Notice how a student did this in the notes in exercise G.

Peleg 3D Printing [notes while listening]
At design school—Peleg decided to print collection from home.
Main ideas [notes after listening]

WORDS IN THE TALK
fabrics and *textiles* (n): cloth
filament (n): a plastic material used by 3D printers
internship (n): a job that provides work experience
open-source file (n): free computer code

G ▶**1.17** **WATCH FOR DETAILS** Read one student's notes on segment 2 of Peleg's edited TED Talk. Then watch the segment. Complete the student's notes as you watch.

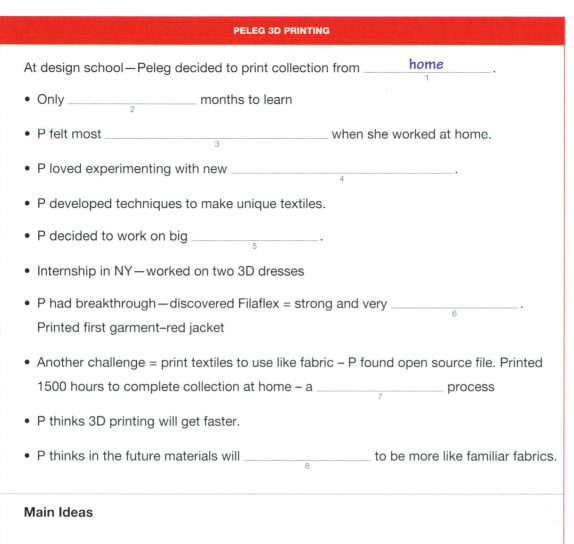

PELEG 3D PRINTING

At design school—Peleg decided to print collection from ___*home*___ .
1

- Only _____ months to learn
  2

- P felt most _____ when she worked at home.
  3

- P loved experimenting with new _____ .
  4

- P developed techniques to make unique textiles.

- P decided to work on big _____ .
  5

- Internship in NY—worked on two 3D dresses

- P had breakthrough—discovered Filaflex = strong and very _____ .
  6
  Printed first garment–red jacket

- Another challenge = print textiles to use like fabric – P found open source file. Printed 1500 hours to complete collection at home – a _____ process
  7

- P thinks 3D printing will get faster.

- P thinks in the future materials will _____ to be more like familiar fabrics.
  8

Main Ideas

H REVIEW NOTES FOR MAIN IDEAS Review the notes in exercise G. Check [✓] the the two sentences below that best express the main ideas of the talk.

1. ☐ The way we get our clothing will change.

2. ☐ Everyone should print their own clothes.

3. ☐ Peleg made a skirt overnight.

4. ☐ Peleg believes that the future of fashion will include 3D printing.

5. ☐ Current fashion design will disappear.

I Write the sentences you chose in exercise H at the bottom of the notes in exercise G on page 77. Compare your answers with a partner's.

J ▶ **1.18 EXPAND YOUR VOCABULARY** Watch the excerpts from the TED Talk. Guess the meanings of the phrases in the box.

> move on   actually   24-7   in no time

K WATCH MORE Go to TED.com to watch the full TED Talk by Danit Peleg.

AFTER YOU WATCH

L COMMUNICATE Work with a small group. Discuss these questions.

> A: *One of the advantages of 3D printing is that you can get clothes that fit you perfectly.*
>
> B: *Good point!*

1. Peleg says that 3D printing will allow for more personalized clothing. Explain what you think she means by this.

2. What do you think are some advantages of 3D printing for customers?

3. If printing clothes becomes widespread, how do you think clothing designers, manufacturers, and stores might be affected?

M THINK CRITICALLY Reflect. Work with a partner. Discuss these questions.

1. Do you think that people will download and print their own clothes in the future? Why, or why not?

2. What suggestions would you give to Peleg for clothes that you would like to wear?

Put It Together

A **THINK CRITICALLY** **Synthesize.** Work in small groups. How are the sneakerhead market and Peleg's idea about 3D printing similar? In what ways are they different? Complete the chart and then explain your answers.

	COLLECTABLE SNEAKERS	3D-PRINTED CLOTHES
Uses technology in production or sales		
Famous people design or sell product	✓	✗
Products are widely available		
Products are high-end fashion		
The market can be profitable		
Product allows people to express their own sense of style		

B **THINK CRITICALLY** **Analyze.** Work with a partner. Discuss these questions.

1. Do your fashion choices (clothing, shoes, hair, jewelry, etc.) express your personal identity? Explain your answer.

2. How do you think that collecting sneakers or wearing 3D clothes allows people to express their personal identity?

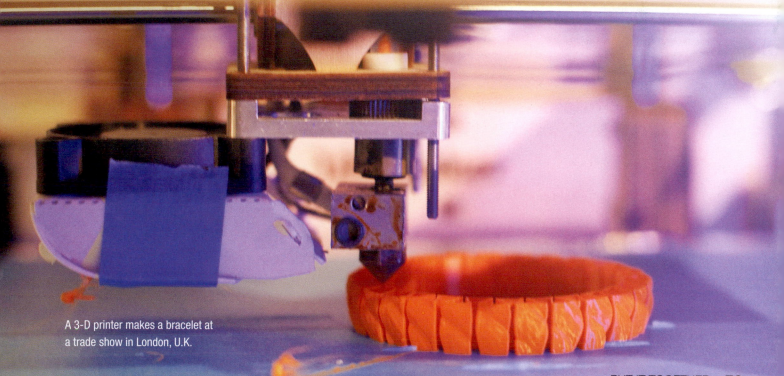

A 3-D printer makes a bracelet at a trade show in London, U.K.

COMMUNICATE

ASSIGNMENT: Interview a Partner Imagine you work for a fashion company that wants to understand what trends are popular and why. You and a partner are going to interview another classmate about his or her opinions on recent fashion trends. Review the ideas in Parts 1 and 2 and the listening and speaking skills as you prepare your presentation.

PREPARE

PRESENTATION SKILL Prepare for an Interview

Sometimes a presenter interviews another person as part of a presentation. This person could be a guest expert, someone from the audience, or a colleague. The speaker may interview this person to help explain or illustrate important ideas.

When you interview someone in a presentation, consider these points:

- Ask open questions, that is, questions that begin with *What, How,* and *Why,* instead of *yes/no* questions. This will make the interview more interesting.

- Be sure your questions are clearly worded so the other person—or the audience—doesn't get confused.

- Avoid looking at your notes or thinking about your next question when the person is talking.

- Pay attention to the person's answer. You may need to ask a follow-up question to get a clearer answer.

C With your partner, follow the steps below to prepare for your interview.

1. Write two questions to ask about a fashion trend. For example, you could ask about:
   - popular clothing brands
   - popular places to shop
   - popular hair styles or colors

2. Write two questions that ask for more details about the trend. For example, you could ask about:
   - a personal experience with this trend
   - an opinion about the trend
   - a prediction about the trend

D Decide who will ask each question and who will write down the answers.

E Read the rubric on page 180 before you conduct your interview. Notice how your interview will be evaluated. Keep these categories in mind as you present and watch your classmates' presentations.

PRESENT

F Ask someone from another group for an interview. Interview that person in front of your class. Watch your classmates' interviews.

G **THINK CRITICALLY** **Evaluate.** Discuss your feedback in a small group. Decide the two things you did well and two areas for improvement.

REFLECT

Reflect on what you have learned. Check [✓] your progress.

I can
- ☐ make and confirm predictions.
- ☐ make suggestions.
- ☐ pronounce numbers.
- ☐ review my notes.
- ☐ prepare for an interview.

I understand the meanings of these words and can use them.
Circle those you know. Underline those you need to work on.

accelerate	demonstrate AWL	market	significantly AWL
assemble AWL	dominant AWL	modify AWL	supply
breakthrough	empower	primary AWL	version AWL
classic AWL	evolve AWL	profile	widespread AWL
demand	flexible AWL	release AWL	weird

Engineered
by Nature

THINK AND DISCUSS

1 Study the photo and read the caption. How might this swimsuit be better than other swimsuits?

2 Read the unit title. Why do you think engineers want to copy designs from nature?

An Olympic swimmer in a swimsuit made of fabric based on shark skin

PART 1   The Science of Surfaces

BEFORE YOU LISTEN

A **COMMUNICATE** Work with a partner. Look at the photo. How would you describe shark skin?

B 🎧 **2.2** **THINK CRITICALLY** **Predict.** You are going to hear a documentary about how scientists copy nature to create new products. Listen to the beginning of the documentary. Then discuss these questions with a partner.

  1. Why do you think scientists are interested in shark skin?

  2. What do you think they can learn from it?

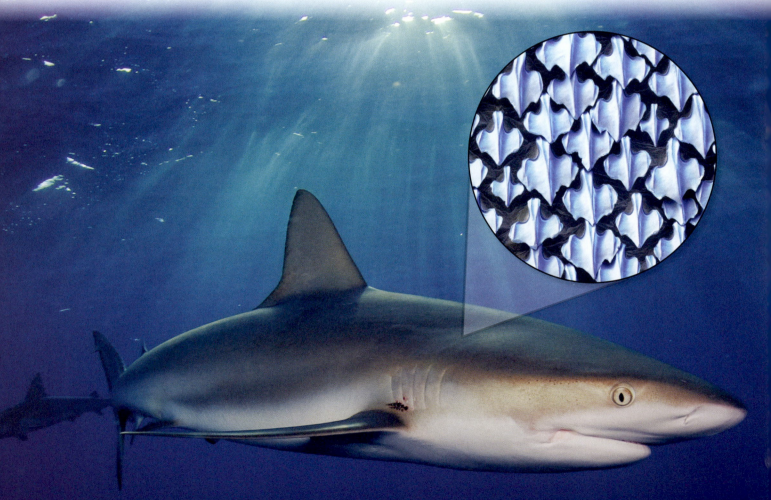

Scientists have studied the scales
on a shark's skin.

VOCABULARY

C **2.3** Read and listen to the sentences with words from the documentary. Guess the meanings of the words in bold. Then choose the correct meanings.

1. There is a **layer** of thin ice on the top of the lake. It is dangerous to walk on it.

   A **layer** is a:
   - **a.** sheet; covering
   - **b.** piece
   - **c.** type; kind

2. This animal catches its food in a **unique** way. I've never seen anything like it.

   Unique means:
   - **a.** frightening
   - **b.** strange; difficult to understand
   - **c.** one of a kind; very unusual

3. A bird's feathers have several **functions.** They keep the bird warm and they help it to fly.

   Function means:
   - **a.** origin
   - **b.** purpose
   - **c.** design

4. There are thousands of **organisms** in the world, from tiny bacteria to animals as large as whales.

   Organisms are:
   - **a.** living things
   - **b.** parts of the body
   - **c.** diseases

5. Mathematics has many practical **applications** in everyday life, for example, in managing your money.

   An **application** is a/an:
   - **a.** factor
   - **b.** use
   - **c.** explanation

6. There is ice on the ground so it is very **slippery.** Be careful and walk slowly.

   Slippery means:
   - **a.** dangerous
   - **b.** making things very cold
   - **c.** causing things to slide or fall

7. The author **adapted** the story so that young children could understand it.

   Adapt means:
   - **a.** to improve
   - **b.** to change for different conditions
   - **c.** to use again

8. The screen of the cell phone was protected by a clear plastic **film.**

   A **film** is a:
   - **a.** thin covering
   - **b.** hard case
   - **c.** liquid

9. The scientists needed a powerful microscope to see the complex **structure** inside the tiny bacteria.

   Structure means:
   - **a.** use; purpose
   - **b.** behavior
   - **c.** arrangement; design

10. When there is no wind, the **surface** of the water is smooth.

    The **surface** is the:
    - **a.** top part
    - **b.** color
    - **c.** temperature

D COMMUNICATE Write an example of each of the following. Then compare your answers with a partner.

> A: *I went on a cruise to the Antarctic.*
> B: *Really! What a **unique** experience.*

1. A **unique** experience you had on vacation

_____

2. A practical **application** of something you learned in high school

_____

3. One **function** of the human tongue

_____

4. A story or book that has been **adapted** for a movie

_____

5. A **slippery surface**

_____

6. Something that has **layers**

_____

LISTEN

E **2.4** **1.19** **LISTEN FOR MAIN IDEAS** Read the statements below. Then listen to the documentary. Use three of the vocabulary items from exercise C to complete the statements about the main ideas of the documentary.

1. Many organisms have _____ surface structures.

2. Each surface has a special _____ that is important for the organism.

3. Scientists and engineers can _____ the structures found in nature for other applications.

F **CONFIRM PREDICTIONS** Work with a partner. Review your predictions from exercise B on page 84. Discuss whether your predictions were correct.

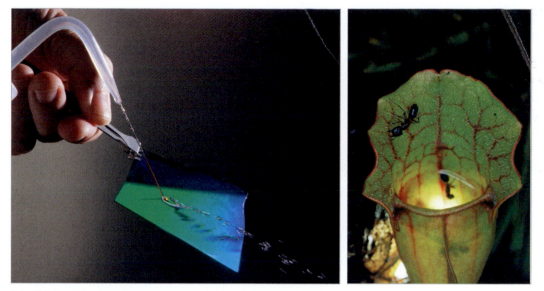

Scientists have developed a material based on the surface structure of the pitcher plant.

LISTENING SKILL Recognize References to Key Terms

Most speakers refer to key terms several times during a lecture or presentation. They may repeat words and phrases exactly, but sometimes they refer to the same term in different ways. For example, they use synonyms or phrases with similar meanings. Notice the reference to the key term "adapt" in the following example:

> Some lizards **can adapt to** their surroundings by changing their skin color. This **ability to change** helps them survive.

Listening for these key terms can help you understand what the speaker thinks is most important.

G 🎧 **2.5** **LISTEN FOR KEY TERMS** Work with a partner. One of the key terms the presenter talks about is *surfaces*. Read the excerpts below. Then listen to segment 1. Complete each excerpt with words that repeat or refer to this key term.

1. "Right, so what do I mean by _____surfaces_____? Well, your skin is a natural
   ₁

   surface—a _____ that _____ your whole body."
   ₂   ₃

2. "The shark's _____ has a unique structure. It is covered with a
   ₄

   _____ of tiny scales in the shape of a diamond."
   ₅

3. "Engineers adapted the structure of shark skin and created a thin

   _____ that can be used on walls, floors, and
   ₆

   other _____."
   ₇

Take Notes Using Key Terms

When you listen to a lecture or presentation, you can organize your notes around key terms. The first time you listen, notice the different words and phrases that refer to the key terms. Write the key terms down and leave space underneath them. When you listen a second time, listen for details about these key terms and take notes underneath them.

KEY TERM 1	KEY TERM 2	KEY TERM 3
details	details	details

H **2.6** **LISTEN FOR DETAILS** Listen to segments 1 and 2 of the documentary. Complete the notes with details based on the key terms.

Segment 1

SURFACE	FUNCTION	APPLICATION
shark has tiny _____ ; 1 _____ 2 shape	prevents growth of _____ 3	film on _____ , 4 floors, and other surfaces

Segment 2

SURFACE	FUNCTION	APPLICATION
pitcher plant rough when _____ 5 slippery when _____ 6	catches food; causes _____ to 7 fall into pitcher and die	slippery film that prevents anything from _____ to it 8

AFTER YOU LISTEN

I **THINK CRITICALLY** **Reflect.** Work with a partner. Each of the biomimicry projects in the documentary began with an observation by a scientist. What were the scientists' observations for the shark and the pitcher plant? Complete each statement.

1. For sharks, the scientists observed that _____

   _____ .

2. For pitcher plants, the scientists observed that _____

   _____ .

J **THINK CRITICALLY** **Apply.** Work in a small group. Describe an observation that you can make about a different plant or an animal, such as how a cheetah runs or the way an octopus moves through the water. Think about an application this could have if scientists and engineers were able to adapt this for a new purpose.

    A: *I've noticed that the plants in my apartment always turn toward the sun. So, is there a way scientists could adapt this function?*

    B: *Well, there could be applications for solar energy. What if solar panels could automatically turn toward the sun?*

Photovoltaic solar panels rotating toward the sun

SPEAKING

SPEAKING SKILL Use Signal Words to Mark Transitions

Speakers often use signal words such as *now, right, so,* and *well* to get their listeners' attention. Then speakers may transition (move on) to do one of the following:

1. Introduce a new topic

   Now/Right/So/Well, let's look at some of the research I am doing.

2. Expand or explain a topic they have introduced

   Now/Right/So/Well, what's the best way to solve this problem?

3. Sum up what they have said

   Well/So, that's how I see it.

Signal words also give listeners an extra moment to process what they have just heard. When you are speaking, you can help your listeners by pausing briefly after you use one of these signal words.

(See page 165 in the *Independent Student Handbook* for more information on signal words.)

K **COLLABORATE** Work with a partner. Read the excerpts below from the documentary. Underline the signal words in each. Then choose the reason why the speaker made each transition.

1. *"This week, we are going to look at how scientists and engineers are adapting the surfaces of plants and animals for new purposes. Right, so what do I mean by surfaces? Well, your skin is a natural surface—a layer that covers your whole body."*

   a. introduce a new topic

   b. expand or explain current topic

   c. sum up

2. *"So, let's start with the shark. The shark's skin has a unique structure."*

   a. introduce a new topic

   b. expand or explain current topic

   c. sum up

3. *"The film helps prevent the growth of bacteria. Now, let's move to the world of plants. Most plants use air, water, and sunlight to make their own food."*

   a. introduce a new topic

   b. explain or expand current topic

   c. sum up

4. *"Just think of all the uses this could have! So, these are just two examples of biomimicry and how scientists and engineers can adapt designs from nature to improve our lives."*

   a. introduce a new topic

   b. explain or expand current topic

   c. sum up

PRONUNCIATION SKILL **Linking Sounds**

Speakers often link the sound at the end of one word to the sound at the beginning of the next word. This makes their speech sound smooth and fluent.

If the end of one word is a consonant sound and the sound at the beginning of the next word is a vowel, it often sounds as if the consonant begins the next word (e.g., *think of = thin-kof*). If the consonant sound at the end of one word is the same as the beginning of the next, the consonant is pronounced just once and held a little longer (e.g., *insectsslide.*). Listen to the examples below:

2.7

people are ➔ *peepe-lar*   *because of* ➔ *becau-zuv*

scared of ➔ *scare-duv*   *shark's skin* ➔ *shark-sskin*

Most people are scared of sharks because of their large, sharp teeth.

L **2.8** Draw link marks according to the examples in the skill box in the excerpt below. Then listen and check your answers.

   "The shark's skin has a unique structure. It is covered with a layer of tiny scales in the shape of a diamond."

M Work with a partner. Take turns saying the excerpt from exercise L. Link the sounds that you marked. Listen to your partner and check that he or she links the sounds correctly.

learnmore People have been copying designs from nature for centuries. Leonardo da Vinci (1452–1519) was one of the first biomimicry inventors. He designed a "flying machine" based on observations of birds and how they flew.

N **THINK CRITICALLY** **Interpret an Infographic.** Work with a partner. Study the infographic below. Then answer the questions.

1. The biomimicry projects in the documentary are based on the surface structure of the organisms. What feature are the biomimicry projects below based on?

2. How do you think the Kingfisher's beak helps it survive?

3. What is another possible application for the mosquito's proboscis?

THE BULLET TRAIN

INSPIRATION: The Kingfisher

FUNCTIONS: Beak doesn't make a large splash when entering water

APPLICATION: A train with a long nose that makes the train less noisy

THE HYPODERMIC NEEDLE

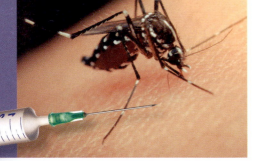

INSPIRATION: The mosquito

FUNCTIONS: Mosquito's thin proboscis (nose) makes its "bite" almost painless

APPLICATION: A proposed design for a needle that you can't feel!

THE BIONIC CAR

INSPIRATION: The Boxfish

FUNCTIONS: Boxfish's body moves easily through water

APPLICATION: The car moves more easily through air

Why I make robots the size of a grain of rice

> **"** Imagine what you could do if you had robots that could swim through your blood. **"**

BEFORE YOU WATCH

A **THINK CRITICALLY** **Predict.** Work with a partner. Read the title of Sarah Bergbreiter's TED Talk and the information about her below. What possible applications might micro-robots have?

B Read the following statements. Choose the number that you think makes each statement true. After you watch the talk, check your answers.

1. Micro-robots can jump (10 / 100 / 1,000) times higher than their size.

2. Some micro-robots weigh only (3 / 30 / 300) milligrams.

SARAH BERGBREITER Micro-roboticist

Sarah Bergbreiter is an engineer who uses advanced technology to design tiny robots—micro-robots—that can run, roll, and jump high into the air. Many are only a few millimeters long.

Bergbreiter's idea worth spreading is that robots the size of insects may have widespread and very useful applications.

VOCABULARY

c 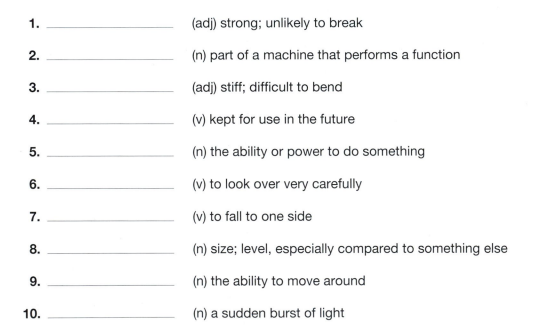 **2.9** The sentences below will help you learn words in the TED Talk. Read and listen to the sentences. Guess the meanings of the words in bold. Then match each word to its definition.

a. The robots used electricity that is **stored** in small batteries.

b. You need to use **rigid** building material. If you use something soft, the structure cannot stand.

c. We need to **inspect** every part of the machine to make sure it is safe to operate.

d. Adding more legs improved the robot's **mobility.** It can now move faster and more easily.

e. We made a model of the robot on a small **scale** before we started building the full-size version.

f. The robot has a **mechanism** that makes it jump really high.

g. When the robot's main light switched on, it gave off a **flash** of light.

h. Ants have the **capability** of carrying something that weighs more than they do.

i. If you put too many heavy things on one side of the cart, it will **tip over.**

j. The machine is very **robust.** It works even in difficult conditions.

1. _____	(adj) strong; unlikely to break
2. _____	(n) part of a machine that performs a function
3. _____	(adj) stiff; difficult to bend
4. _____	(v) kept for use in the future
5. _____	(n) the ability or power to do something
6. _____	(v) to look over very carefully
7. _____	(v) to fall to one side
8. _____	(n) size; level, especially compared to something else
9. _____	(n) the ability to move around
10. _____	(n) a sudden burst of light

WORDS IN THE TALK
locomotion (n): movement
rubble (n): broken bits of bricks from destroyed buildings

D **COMMUNICATE** Work with a partner. Take turns answering the questions.

1. Where is the safest place to **store** important personal information?

2. What steps has your school or college taken to help people with limited **mobility?**

3. What do you think is a computer's most important **capability?**

4. The **scale** of electronics such as cell phones has gotten smaller and smaller. Now some of them are going in the other direction. What size do you prefer for a cell phone, and why?

WATCH

E ▶ **1.20** **WATCH FOR MAIN IDEAS** Watch Bergbreiter's edited TED Talk. Check [✓] the two most important ideas that Bergbreiter wants her audience to understand.

1. ☐ The scale of robots is getting smaller every year.

2. ☐ Micro-robots have many possible applications.

3. ☐ Micro-robots of the future will be semi-intelligent.

4. ☐ Engineering mobility on a small scale is a big challenge.

Bergbreiter and her students engineer micro-robots to move like ants.

F ▶ **1.21 RECOGNIZE KEY TERMS** One of Bergbreiter's key terms is *mobility*. Watch and complete the excerpts below with different words and phrases that refer to this key term.

Segment 1

1. *"First of all, how do we get the capabilities of an ant in a robot at the same size scale? Well, first we need to figure out how to make them _____ when they're so small."*

2. *"I'll start with _____. Insects _____ around amazingly well. This video is from UC Berkeley. It shows a cockroach moving over incredibly rough terrain without tipping over."*

3. *"_____ is another really interesting way to _____ when you're very small."*

Segment 2

4. *"So, the next video is one of my favorites. So you have this 300-mg robot _____ about eight centimeters in the air."*

5. *"So, I think you can imagine all the cool things that we could do with robots that can _____ and _____ and _____ and _____ at this size scale."*

G UNDERSTAND TRANSITIONS Read the excerpts from Bergbreiter's talk. Underline each signal word. Choose the reason she made each transition.

1. *"To make these things really functional, we want a lot of them working together in order to do bigger things. So, I'll start with mobility. Insects move around amazingly well."*
   a. to introduce a new topic
   b. to explain or expand current topic
   c. to sum up

2. *"And the basic idea is that we're going to compress this, store energy in the springs, and then release it to jump. So, there's no motors on board this right now, no power."*
   a. to introduce a new topic
   b. to explain or expand current topic
   c. to sum up

3. *"So, I think I've given you some of the possibilities of what we can do with these small robots."*
   a. introduce a new topic
   b. explain or expand current topic
   c. sum up

H ▶ `1.22` **WATCH FOR DETAILS** Watch segments 3 and 4 of the talk and complete the notes with details.

Segment 3

Intro:

- Bergbreiter and students work on _____ robots
  ₁

- Think of robotic versions of _____
  ₂

- Challenge = get capabilities of ant in robot same _____ scale
  ₃

Segment 4

Contributions from B's lab:

- Combine _____ and _____ materials in small mechanism
  ₄   ₅

  - _____ material = silicon
    ₆

  - _____ material = silicon rubber
    ₇

- No _____ on board, no power
  ₈

What we could do with micro-robots:

- After natural disastors, look for _____
  ₉

- Inspect _____ to make sure it's _____
  ₁₀   ₁₁

- They could operate without having to _____ you open
  ₁₂

I ▶ **1.23** **EXPAND YOUR VOCABULARY** Watch the excerpts from the TED Talk. Guess the meanings of the phrases in the box.

> figure out   semi-intelligent   rough terrain   set off   destination

J **WATCH MORE** Go to TED.com to watch the full TED Talk by Sarah Bergbreiter.

AFTER YOU WATCH

K **THINK CRITICALLY** **Infer.** Work with a partner. Read the excerpt from the TED Talk. Then discuss your answers to the questions.

> *"And we've made some advances so far, but there's still a long way to go, and hopefully some of you can contribute to that destination."*

1. What does Bergbreiter mean by "there's still a long way to go"?

2. What does she mean by "contribute"?

L **COMMUNICATE** Work with a partner. Discuss the questions below.

1. Read the possible applications for micro-robots below. Check [✓] the ones you think are the most useful.

a. ☐ Tasks that are dangerous

b. ☐ Tasks that require absolutely perfect performance every time

c. ☐ Tasks that are too complex for humans

d. ☐ Tasks that are very repetitive

e. ☐ Tasks that are in spaces too small for humans

f. ☐ Other: _____

2. Which jobs do you think could be most affected by the use of micro-robots?

An artist's impression of micro-robots working in someone's blood stream

Put It Together

A **THINK CRITICALLY** **Synthesize.** Work in small groups. In what ways are the biomimicry projects in Parts 1 and 2 similar? Check [✓] the boxes in the chart. Then explain your answers to members of the group by giving examples from the two presentations.

> A: *The projects in Parts 1 and 2 are both inspired by nature.*
> B: *Right. They were inspired by plants or animals.*

	"SHARK SKIN" FILM	NON-STICK FILM	MICRO-ROBOTS
inspired by nature	✓	✓	✓
works on a very small scale			
focuses on mobility			
focuses on surface structure			
many possible applications			
applications already in use			

B **COMMUNICATE** Work with a partner. Which of the biomimicry projects from this unit do you think are the most useful? Explain your answer.

> A: *I think the hypodermic needle is the most useful.*
> B: *I agree. I hate getting shots!*

COMMUNICATE

ASSIGNMENT: Group Presentation Your group is going to give a presentation about another application for one of the projects you learned about in Parts 1 and 2. Review the ideas, vocabulary, and skills in the unit as you prepare for your presentation.

PREPARE

> **PRESENTATION SKILL** **Have a Strong Ending**
>
> It is important to have a strong ending to your presentation so that your audience will remember your ideas. You can summarize what you have said to make your point clear. You can also connect key ideas to your audience in a concrete way. It is not a good idea to introduce any new ideas in the conclusion. Notice how Bergbreiter ends by summarizing briefly and asking her audience to get involved.
>
> ▶ **1.24** *"So, I think I've given you some of the possibilities of what we can do with these small robots. And we've made some advances so far, but there's still a long way to go, and hopefully some of you can contribute to that destination."*

(See page 174 of the *Independent Student Handbook* for more information on having a strong ending.)

C Work with your group. Use the information and questions below to brainstorm other applications for the projects you have learned about. Do not worry about whether the idea is technically possible yet. Write short notes about your ideas.

- The "shark skin" film prevents bacteria from growing. How could this be used? Where would it be useful?

- The non-stick film is slippery; in other words, ice, oil, paint, etc. will not stick to it. How could this be used? Where would it be useful?

- Micro-robots may be better for some jobs than humans. What kinds of jobs might these be?

D **COLLABORATE** Choose one of the ideas you brainstormed in exercise C. In your group, discuss who will do the following parts of your presentation. Remember to repeat key words and use signals words and pauses to mark transitions.

- Explain how nature inspired this project:

- Review your notes from Part 1 (page 88) or Part 2 (pages 96–97).
- Be sure you can explain the key ideas.
- Consider showing a photo or diagram of the plant or animal.

- Explain your application:
  - Explain the connection between the original research and your idea.
  - Describe how your idea will work.

- Give a short conclusion:
  - Explain why your application is useful and important.
  - Restate the importance of learning from nature.

E Read the rubric on page 181 before you present. Notice how your presentation will be evaluated. Keep these categories in mind as you present and watch your classmates' presentations.

PRESENT

F Give your presentation to a small group. Watch your classmates' presentations. After you watch each one, provide feedback using the rubric as a guide. Add notes or any other feedback you want to share.

G **THINK CRITICALLY** **Evaluate.** As a class, discuss what each presenter did well and what might make each presentation even stronger. Decide the two things you did well, and two areas for improvement.

REFLECT

Reflect on what you have learned. Check [✓] your progress.

I can
- ☐ recognize references to key terms.
- ☐ take notes using key terms.
- ☐ use signal words to mark transitions.
- ☐ link sounds.
- ☐ end strong.

I understand the meanings of these words and can use them.
Circle those you know. Underline those you need to work on.

adapt AWL	function AWL	organism	store
application	inspect AWL	rigid AWL	structure AWL
capability AWL	layer AWL	robust	surface
film	mechanism AWL	scale	tip over
flash	mobility	slippery	unique AWL

Lending a Hand

An organization in Rajat, India, teaches women the skills to build and repair solar-powered lanterns.

THINK AND DISCUSS

1 Look at the photo and read the caption. How do you think the lives of these women have changed?

2 Read the unit title. What do you think "lending a hand" means?

Microloans: Breaking the Cycle of Poverty

BEFORE YOU LISTEN

A **THINK CRITICALLY** **Predict.** Work with a partner. The title of Part 1 is "Microloans: Breaking the Cycle of Poverty." Look at the photo and read the caption. Discuss these questions.

1. The expression "cycle of poverty" suggests that some people cannot get out of poverty. Why do you think it's hard to break the cycle of poverty?

2. A loan is money that you borrow and then have to pay back later. What do you think a microloan is?

3. How do you think microloans can help the people of the Gulu District break the cycle of poverty?

The Cycle of Poverty
Poverty is the state of being very poor. In the Gulu District in Uganda, many people have to survive on less than $1.25 a day. Without access to money and education, many families get trapped in a cycle of poverty that can last for generations.

A restaurant owner stands at a table in the Gulu District of Uganda. Her business was started with a microloan.

VOCABULARY

B 🎧 **2.10** Read and listen to these sentences with words from the lecture you will hear. Guess the meanings of the words in bold. Then match each word to its definition.

a. This medicine is not making the patient better. We need to find one that is more **effective.**

b. People do not earn a lot of money in Uganda. The average **income** is less than $500 dollars a year.

c. This test is a **measure** of how well the students have learned the material.

d. We bought the building for $30,000 and sold it for $45,000, so we made a 50 percent **profit.**

e. Many people lost their homes in the earthquake. Several organizations are providing **aid** to these families.

f. World Bank **records** show that almost 13 percent of the world's population earned less than two dollars a day in 2012.

g. He is trying to become **financially** independent. He does not want to rely on his family for money.

h. When you borrow money from the bank, you have to pay it back with **interest**— an added fee for borrowing the money.

i. Many young adults **depend on** their parents until they can find a job.

j. He asked his friends to **invest** money in his new business. Now that the business is successful, he has paid them back.

1. _____ (n) help

2. _____ (v) have need of support

3. _____ (adj) having a good result

4. _____ (adv) related to the management of money

5. _____ (n) money that you earn from working

6. _____ (n) a way of evaluating something

7. _____ (n) the percentage of money you pay for a loan

8. _____ (v) put money into a business

9. _____ (n) written information that shows that something happened

10. _____ (n) the money that you get when you sell something for a higher price than you paid

C COMMUNICATE Work with a partner and discuss these questions. Use the words or phrases in bold in your answers.

> A: *I think it's better to borrow money from a bank. It's more official.*
> B: *Yes, though I depend on my family to give me money.*

1. Do you think it is a good idea to borrow money from a bank? Or is it better to **depend on** friends or family members for a loan? Explain your answer.

2. If you could **invest** in a business, what kind of business would you invest in? Why do you think it would be **financially** successful?

3. Is profit the only **measure** of success for a business? Why, or why not?

4. What do you think is the most **effective** way to organize and keep **records** of how much you make and spend?

LISTEN

D 🎧 **2.11** ▶ **1.25** **LISTEN FOR MAIN IDEAS** Listen to each segment of the lecture. Choose the statement that best expresses the speaker's main idea in each segment.

Segment 1

_____ **1.** Many people in the world live in poverty.

_____ **2.** The interest on microloans is very low.

_____ **3.** Microloans can help people in poverty.

Segment 2

_____ **1.** Education offers the best way out of poverty.

_____ **2.** Education can make microloans more effective.

_____ **3.** Microloans are not as effective as some aid agencies say they are.

A small business owner selling produce she has grown in the Gulu Distract of Uganda

When you take notes on a talk or lecture, you don't have time to write all the speaker's words. You can save time if you use symbols to show the relationships among ideas. Here are some common symbols and what they might mean in your notes:

–   between, from...to

=   is, are, equals

≠   isn't, aren't, does not equal

>   more than, bigger than

<   less than, smaller than

→   cause, lead to, come before

"More than 50 percent of the population of Gulu lives below the international poverty line."

Notes: **> 50% live in poverty**

E   **2.12 LISTEN FOR DETAILS** Read the notes below. Then listen to segment 1 of the lecture and complete the notes with the correct symbols.

What is Gulu like?

_____ 50% live in poverty

  1

> half _____ farmers

       2

How do microloans work for Gulu farmers?

Microloans _____ regular bank loans; collateral (house) not needed

           3

Loans $50 _____ $100; no collateral needed

          4

Interest rates _____ 35%

         5

After microloans _____ farmers invest in farms

           6

_____ bigger profits

  7

Part of the profits _____ payment of loan

            8

LISTENING SKILL Recognize Facts and Opinions

It is important to recognize the difference between facts and opinions. A speaker often supports his or her opinion with facts and other information. Listening for the following phrases will help you recognize facts and opinions.

OPINIONS	FACTS
I think . . . *I believe . . .* *I'm pretty sure . . .* *In my opinion/view . . .*	*There is evidence/proof . . .* *Experts claim/argue . . .* *Studies show . . .* *Researchers found . . .* *The record shows . . .*

F 🎧 **2.13** Listen to segment 2 of the lecture. Write the missing word(s) in the excerpts below.

1. *"I have given money to organizations that make microloans. _____ they are the most effective way to help poor people."*

2. *"That depends on your what your measure is. There is some evidence of success. First, _____ that borrowers almost always pay back the loans."*

3. *"Borrowers almost always pay back the loans—about 95 percent. In addition, _____ by researchers at the Massachusetts Institute of Technology _____ that microloans help one group the most: people who already own a business."*

4. *"No, I wouldn't, because _____ such small amounts of money can make much of a difference."*

5. *"Well, you are right. These _____ that the loans resulted in no change in the usual measures of poverty."*

6. *"There is another way to look at the situation, though. Although economic experts do _____ that people in poverty often remain poor after they take out a microloan, the same _____ also _____ that loans allow the families to become more financially stable."*

7. *"_____ aid suggests that this kind of support increases the chance that microloans will help people break the cycle of poverty."*

G Review the sentences in exercise F. Write *F* next to the facts, and *O* next to opinions.

AFTER YOU LISTEN

H **THINK CRITICALLY** **Analyze.** Work with a partner. Complete the sentences with information from the lecture.

1. What are three ways in which microloans have been successful?

   a. Ninety-five percent of borrowers

   _____ .

   b. Microloans help people who

   _____ to get ahead.

   c. Microloans help poor families become

   _____ .

2. In what way can microloans be considered a failure? Discuss with your partner.

A vendor selling produce at a farm stand supported by Community Action Fund for Women in Africa

A goat purchased through Community Action Fund for Women in Africa

How Microloans Helped Women in Gulu

I THINK CRITICALLY Interpret a Graphic. Work with a partner. Look at the graphic above. Put the steps below in the correct order and discuss how microloans helped the women of Gulu break the cycle of poverty.

a. _____ saved money

b. _____ used profits to help their community

c. _____ repaid the microloans

d. _____ got training in good farming practices

e. _____ took classes in math and reading

f. __1__ got microloans

SPEAKING

SPEAKING SKILL Express an Opinion

It is important to be able to state your opinion clearly and effectively. Use the phrases you heard in the Listening Skill to give an opinion:

I think…   I (don't) believe…   In my view…

To state an even stronger opinion you can use these phrases:

I strongly believe that…   I am certain that…   It is very clear that…

Remember, in academic situations it is important to give facts or other specific information that support your opinion.

"I have given money to organizations that make microloans. I have read reports that they are the most effective way to help poor people."

J COMMUNICATE Work with a small group. Read about three people who want to take out a microloan. With your group, decide who should get the loan. Any of them would be a good choice, but you can only choose one. Use expressions of opinion.

NAME Esperanza

STATUS Married with two children

COUNTRY Peru

WANTS $600 to buy wool to knit hats and gloves that she will sell in her husband's store

ADDITIONAL INFO First microloan request

NAME Thuy

STATUS Married with two adult children

COUNTRY Vietnam

WANTS $750 to buy baby fish to expand their fish farm

ADDITIONAL INFO Second microloan request. Started fish farm with the first request ($450) two years ago, which was paid back with interest.

NAME Hector

STATUS Married with six children

COUNTRY El Salvador

WANTS $350 to buy new fishing nets and repair his boat

ADDITIONAL INFO First microloan request

K THINK CRITICALLY Reflect. Think about your discussion in exercise J. Check [✓] which factors were the most important to you when you made your decision.

_____ Amount of loan   _____ Purpose of loan   _____ Size of family

_____ Other _____

A thought group is a group of words that go together to form a thought or idea. In writing, we often use commas or other punctuation to show where our thoughts begin and end. Speakers do this by pausing briefly between thought groups. This makes it easier for listeners to understand them.

These types of phrases often form thought groups:

Verb phrases: *buy a house; pay it back*

Prepositional phrases: *for a profit; in their farms; about 95 percent*

Noun phrases: *researchers at the Massachusetts Institute of Technology*

Introductory phrases: *First of all; So,*

L **2.14** Listen to the excerpt and notice the pauses at the end of each thought group. Then say the lines. Pause very briefly at the end of each thought group.

"So, / what kind of help / did these families get? / They got microloans / from CAFWA. / A microloan is different / from a regular bank loan. / First of all, / the amounts are very low— / usually between 50 and 100 dollars."

M **2.15** Work with a partner. Listen to the excerpt and mark (/) the speaker's thought groups. Then say the lines with brief pauses at the end of each thought group. Take turns listening and checking your partner's pauses.

"Second, the borrowers don't need any collateral. When you borrow money to buy a house, for example, if you don't pay back the loan, the bank will take your house. The house is your collateral. The people in Gulu are too poor to provide collateral. Finally, the interest on a microloan is low enough that most borrowers can pay back the loan— usually between 10 and 30 percent. Before they got the loans, the women in Gulu barely made enough to feed their families. They were in a cycle of poverty."

N With your partner, take turns saying the lines from exercise M, pausing briefly at the end of each thought group.

Should you donate differently?

> **"** What if we use technology to put cash directly into a poor person's hands. **"**

BEFORE YOU WATCH

A Work with a small group. Read the title of the talk and the information about the TED speaker. Then answer the questions.

1. Why do you think Joy Sun was not satisfied with the performance of aid agencies?

2. Do you think donating directly to the poorest people in the world is a better idea than giving to aid agencies? Why, or why not?

JOY SUN   Aid Worker

Joy Sun has worked for different aid agencies that help people in poverty, but she grew dissatisfied with the performance of these agencies, so she helped start *GiveDirectly*. *GiveDirectly* is an organization that lets people donate money directly to the poorest people in the world.

Joy Sun's idea worth spreading is that it may be best to donate money directly to people in poverty instead of giving it to aid organizations. She believes that often people living in poverty know how to use the money most effectively for their own needs.

VOCABULARY

B 🎧 **2.16** The sentences below will help you learn words in the TED Talk. Read and listen to the sentences. Guess the meanings of the words in bold. Then choose the correct meaning.

1. I believe that aid agencies are very effective, but many people believe **otherwise.**

   Otherwise means:

   a. differently   **b.** worse   **c.** falsely

2. The family does not own their home, their farm, or a car. Their only **asset** is a bicycle.

   An **asset** is:

   a. income   **b.** something that makes money   **c.** something of value

3. I am not sure, but I **suspect** that this problem will take a long time to solve.

   Suspect means:

   a. believe but not be certain

   b. understand with difficulty

   c. estimate

4. The two politicians did not want to meet in public, so they passed a message through an **intermediary.**

   An **intermediary** is someone who:

   a. works at about the middle level in a group

   b. decides which group is right

   c. communicates between people or groups

5. There is a **range** of solutions to this problem, from cheap ones to very expensive ones.

   A **range** means:

   a. a variety   **b.** a possibility   **c.** a level

6. The **transfer** of money from her bank to the aid agency took almost a week.

   Transfer means:

   a. delay   **b.** movement   **c.** arrival

7. There is an **assumption** that donating to aid agencies is the best way to help people in poverty.

   Assumption means:

   a. argument

   b. unfair judgment

   c. idea that is not always based on facts

8. I think that we should **reconsider** our original idea now that we know more about the situation.

   Reconsider means:

   a. think about again

   b. revise

   c. state more clearly

9. Phone companies usually add taxes and other **fees** for using a cell phone.

   A **fee** is:

   a. a license   **b.** a cost   **c.** time

10. Many organizations are trying to **figure out** the most effective way to fight poverty.

    Figure out means:

    a. pay for   **b.** choose   **c.** determine

C **COMMUNICATE** Work with a partner. Discuss these statements and questions. Use the words in bold in your discussion.

1. Tell your partner about an **assumption** you made about someone that you later had to **reconsider**.

2. Some people think it is better to **figure out** your problems yourself. Do you agree, or do you think **otherwise?** Explain your point of view to your partner.

3. Describe your most valuable **asset.**

WATCH

D ▶ **1.26** **WATCH FOR MAIN IDEAS** Watch the edited TED Talk. What is the most important idea that Sun wants her audience to understand from her talk?

1. _____ Most aid is like throwing cash out of an airplane.

2. _____ Direct cash transfers work better than other types of donations.

3. _____ We need more evidence to make better decisions about aid.

4. _____ *GiveDirectly* has been very successful.

WORDS IN THE TALK

empirical (adj): based on knowledge or experience of the real world
irony (n): a situation that is the opposite of what you would expect
livestock (n): farm animals
logic (n): a formal and reasoned way of thinking

E ▶ **1.27** **WATCH FOR DETAILS** Watch each segment of Sun's TED Talk. Complete the summary of each segment using a word or phrase from the word bank.

30	1,000	improve	cell phone
poorest	spend	invest	sends money

Segment 1

Sun learned that poor people usually use cash donations

to _____ their lives. For example, in Sri Lanka, men use the
                        1

money to _____ in their businesses. Studies found that people
                        2

do not _____ donations on bad habits like smoking.
                        3

Segment 2

A study in India found that _____ percent of people who
                                            4

received livestock as aid sold it for cash. *GiveDirectly* is the first organization

dedicated to giving cash directly to the poor. It has sent one-time payments of

_____ dollars to families in Uganda and Kenya. Here's how
        5

GiveDirectly works:

1. Target *GiveDirectly* looks for families living in the

_____ villages. They find houses
            6

made of mud and thatch.

2. Check Once a family is chosen, an independent team checks to confirm the family and home are real. They use photos, GPS coordinates, and satellite images to check that it's a real house.

3. Transfer Then *GiveDirectly* sells the family a

_____ . A few weeks later, *GiveDirectly*
            7

_____ to the phone.
        8

F ▶ **1.28** **EXPAND YOUR VOCABULARY** Watch the excerpts from the TED Talk. Guess the meanings of the phrases in the box.

> no strings attached   it turns out   across the board   so-called   show up

G **WATCH MORE** Go to TED.com to watch the full TED Talk by Joy Sun.

AFTER YOU WATCH

H **RECOGNIZE FACTS AND OPINIONS** Read the excerpts below. Underline the signal words and phrases. Then, write F if the statements are *facts* or O if they are *opinions*. Discuss your answers with a partner.

1. "*I believed* I could do more good with money for the poor than the poor could do for themselves." _____O_____

2. "Dozens of studies show that people use cash transfers to improve their own lives." _____

3. "None of these studies found people spend more on drinking or smoking or that people work less." _____

4. "They found that 30 percent of recipients had turned around and sold the livestock they had been given for cash." _____

5. "I believe most aid is better than just throwing money out of a plane." _____

6. "I am absolutely certain that a lot of aid today isn't better than giving directly to the poor." _____

I **THINK CRITICALLY** **Infer.** Read the excerpt from Sun's talk. Why do you think Sun starts her talk with this idea? Is she serious about throwing money out of a plane? Discuss with a partner.

> "I suspect that every aid worker in Africa comes to a time in her career when she wants to take all the money for her project — maybe it's a school or a training program — pack it in a suitcase, get on a plane flying over the poorest villages in the country, and start throwing that money out the window."

Donations used to pay for expenses

Most Aid Agencies

GiveDirectly

50%

15%

For every $100 donated to Give Directly

$8.48
is used for general expenses

$2.99
is used to send money to recipient

$1.79
is used to check on the recipient afterwards

$1.48
is used to identify families

J **THINK CRITICALLY** **Interpret an Infographic.** Work in a small group. In her talk, Sun says that most aid agencies do not give enough of the money they collect to the poor. Study the infographic and answer the questions below.

1. How much of *GiveDirectly*'s donations go to the poor?

2. What is *GiveDirectly*'s largest expense?

3. Why do you think most aid agencies have more expenses than *GiveDirectly*?

4. The amount of money that reaches the poor is just one way to determine if an aid agency is effective. What are some other things to consider?

K **COMMUNICATE** Work with a small group. Read the statements below. Discuss whether or not these are good reasons *not* to make donations. Support your opinions with facts or other evidence wherever you can.

I don't donate money to aid agencies because . . .

. . . the problem is too big. My donation won't make a difference.

. . . I don't have enough money. Someone else should give.

. . . I would rather help people in my own country.

. . . my money will never get to the people who really need it.

. . . ending poverty is the government's job.

A THINK CRITICALLY Synthesize. Work in a small group. Decide if the two types of aid you heard about in Parts 1 and 2 are similar. Complete the chart. Then explain your answers..

MICROLOANS AND DIRECT CASH TRANSFERS	YES OR NO
have similar goals	
use the same technology to deliver donations	
control how money is used by recipients	
provide similar non-financial support to recipients	
help recipients break cycle of poverty	

COMMUNICATE

ASSIGNMENT: Role Play Imagine you have collected $200 to donate to people in need. You will participate in a role play about how to use the money. Review the ideas in Parts 1 and 2, the vocabulary, and the listening, speaking, and pronunciation skills in Part 1 as you prepare for your role play.

PREPARE

PRESENTATION SKILL **Be Personable**

Good presenters try to connect on a personal level with an audience. The audience is more likely to listen, understand, and accept the speaker's message if they feel a connection with him or her. Below are a few ways you can be personable when you present:

- Be warm and friendly.
- Speak simply—write the speech yourself, using words you'd normally use, and imagine that you are having a conversation with the audience.
- Tell relevant stories about how you have engaged with the topic.
- Include stories about real people.
- Show your feelings, especially your enthusiasm or excitement about the topic.

Watch this excerpt from Sun's TED Talk. She tells a relevant story about herself.

▶ **1.29** *"Because to a veteran aid worker, the idea of putting cold, hard cash into the hands of the poorest people on Earth doesn't sound crazy, it sounds really satisfying. I had that moment right about the 10-year mark, and luckily, that's also when I learned that this idea actually exists . . ."*

B COLLABORATE Work in small groups. Read the role cards. Choose a role so that there is at least one student in your group with role A, B, C, and D. Then follow the steps below.

Role A

> You are a fundraiser for *No Strings Attached*. Your job is to ask people for donations.
>
> *No Strings Attached* provides direct cash transfers to families in the poorest countries in sub-Saharan Africa who have experienced many years of war and conflict. They have already helped 15,000 families improve their lives. Eighty-five percent of the money collected goes directly to recipients.

Role B

> You are a fundraiser for the *Microloan Project*. Your job is to ask people for donations.
>
> The *Microloan Project* has been giving microloans of $200–$500 to farmers and small business owners in Haiti since the terrible earthquake in 2010. Haiti is the poorest country in the western hemisphere. Ninety-eight percent of all loans are paid back on time. Ninety percent of the money collected goes directly to recipients.

Role C

> You are a fundraiser for *Give a Goat*. Your job is to ask people for donations.
>
> *Give a Goat* gives people in poverty with no job or special skills a way to improve their lives. The organization gives each family a goat; they can use the goat's milk in two ways. They can use the milk to feed themselves, or they can sell it for cash. When the goat has babies, they can sell the baby goats. People who make donations receive a photo of the family with their new goat and a report on their progress.

Role D

> You have $200 you want to donate. You will ask the fundraisers questions and express your opinion about different forms of giving.

Roles A, B, and C

Decide on how you will convince the donor (Role D) to give money to your aid organization. You will need to:

- introduce your agency: say who you are and what you do.
- respond to questions: giving opinions and using facts from the lecture and TED Talk.
- be personable.

Role D

Decide what information will convince you to donate your money: facts? personal stories? You will need to:

- ask questions about the agency's work and effectiveness.
- express your opinions.
- give reasons why you may not donate (review Part 2, exercise K).

C Read the rubric on page 181 before you present. Notice how your role play will be evaluated. Keep those categories in mind as you present and watch your classmates' presentations.

PRESENT

D Do your role play for the class. Watch your classmates' role plays. After you watch each one, provide feedback using the rubric as a guide. Add notes or any other feedback you want to share.

E **THINK CRITICALLY Evaluate.** In your group, discuss the feedback you received. As a class, discuss what each group did well and what might make each presentation even stronger.

REFLECT

Reflect on what you have learned. Check [✓] your progress.

I can
- ☐ use symbols in my notes.
- ☐ recognize facts and opinions.
- ☐ express an opinion.
- ☐ speak in thought groups.
- ☐ be personable when I present.

I understand the meanings of these words and can use them.
Circle those you know. Underline those you need to work on.

aid AWL	fee AWL	intermediary	range AWL
asset	figure out	invest AWL	reconsider
assumption AWL	financially AWL	measure	record
depend on	income AWL	otherwise	suspect
effective	interest	profit	transfer AWL

Less Is More

A small house in the countryside of Iceland

THINK AND DISCUSS

1 Read the unit title. What do you think "less is more" means?

2 Look at the photo. Would you like to live in this house? Why, or why not?

BEFORE YOU LISTEN

A **COMMUNICATE** Work in a small group. Discuss these questions.

1. Look at the photo. Do you like eating at a place that has many choices on the menu? Why, or why not?

2. Do you think that having more choices is always a good thing? Why, or why not?

B ⌒ **2.17** **COLLABORATE** You are going to listen to a lecture about ideas from a book called *The Paradox of Choice*. A *paradox* is a statement that seems impossible or untrue because it says two opposite things. An example is the title of this unit, *Less Is More*. Listen to segment 1 of the lecture. Then with your group, discuss the meaning of the book title.

Customers have a lot of choices at Cafe Sopra in Sydney, Australia.

VOCABULARY

C 🎧 **2.18** Read and listen to the sentences with words from the lecture. Guess the meanings of the words in bold. Then write each word next to its definition.

a. Social media can **impact** the success of a business. If many people give positive reviews to a product, others are likely to want to buy it.

b. Scientific **research** suggests that people become unhappy if they have too many choices.

c. If you are **aware of** your behavior, you may be able to change it.

d. There are just three **options** at this restaurant: fried chicken, grilled fish, or a veggie burger.

e. **Psychologists** are studying how people react to different kinds of advertisements.

f. Thank you so much! I really **appreciate** all of the help you have given us on this project.

g. Our sales figures have been increasing every month. They are strong **evidence** of the product's popularity.

h. Are you **satisfied** with your new apartment? Is it big enough?

i. An accountant must be a **perfectionist**. Mistakes are not allowed.

j. There are so many choices on the menu! It's so **overwhelming** that I cannot decide.

1. _____ (adj) causing confusion because something is so great in number or effect

2. _____ (n) a person who tries to do things without fault or error

3. _____ (adj) happy with something

4. _____ (n) choices

5. _____ (v) be thankful for

6. _____ (n) information or objects that support the truth

7. _____ (v) have an effect or influence on something

8. _____ (adj) conscious; having knowledge

9. _____ (n) people who study the mind and behavior

10. _____ (n) the detailed study of something

D **COMMUNICATE** Work with a partner. Discuss the questions.

1. Are you a **perfectionist?** Explain why, or why not.

2. Does having a lot of **options impact** your ability to make a decision? Explain why, or why not.

3. Are some kinds of situations **overwhelming** for you? Explain your answer.

4. Are you **satisfied** with the size of your apartment or house? Explain why, or why not.

LISTEN

E 🎧 **2.19** ▶ **1.30** **LISTEN FOR MAIN IDEAS** Read the statements. Then listen to the lecture. Check [✓] the two statements that are true.

1. ☐ People generally believe that more choices are not good.

2. ☐ *The Paradox of Choice* suggests that more choices actually make people less happy.

3. ☐ People in societies with a lot of wealth and freedom are happier today than they were in 1945.

4. ☐ Schwartz thinks that people with a certain kind of personality have a harder time making decisions.

5. ☐ *Maximizer* personality types are usually happier than *Satisficer* personality types.

F 🎧 **2.20** **LISTEN FOR DETAILS** Listen to the first two segments of the lecture. Choose the best word or phrase to complete each statement.

Segment 1

1. The lecture is about how a greater number of choices can have a negative impact on _____ .

    a. happiness   **b.** success   **c.** confusion

2. Yuichi didn't buy an electric toothbrush online because _____ .

    a. there were none that he liked

    b. there were too many choices

    c. he couldn't understand the Web site

3. The book *The Paradox of Choice* by Barry Schwartz says that people think they want _____ choices.

    a. fewer   **b.** more   **c.** better

Segment 2

4. The professor tells the students which _____ has difficulty with decisions.

    a. choice

    b. personality type

    c. number

5. A *satisficer* _____ about things like his or her hair or clothes.

    a. often worries

    b. doesn't care

    c. does not worry much

6. Schwartz says that the *maximizer* has _____ time than a *satisficer* dealing with a lot of choices.

    a. an easier

    b. a better

    c. a harder

7. *Satisficers* have _____ chance of becoming depressed than *maximizers*.

    a. a lower

    b. a greater

    c. the same

Listen for Rhetorical Questions

Sometimes speakers ask a question but do not expect an answer. Often, they even answer the question themselves. This is a **rhetorical question**. Speakers ask rhetorical questions to:

1. signal a central idea, sometimes an idea that they hope listeners will agree with.

    Can money buy happiness?

2. signal that an explanation or more details will follow.

    So, what does this mean? First, . . .

3. engage their listeners and make them feel as if they are interacting with the speaker.

    Have you heard about this?

Listen for rhetorical questions to help you understand what the speaker thinks is important and to follow his or her argument.

G 🎧 **2.21** Work with a partner. Read the questions from the lecture. Then listen to each excerpt and write *R* if the question is rhetorical.

1. _____ *"So, are you saying that people are less happy overall because they have more choices?"*

2. _____ *"What do they mean?"*

3. _____ *"Does anyone here have trouble making a decision when, say, you are at a restaurant or in a store?"*

H THINK CRITICALLY Analyze. Work with a small group. Discuss why you think the professor used each rhetorical question in exercise G. Was it reason 1, 2, or 3 from the Listening Skill box?

A: *I don't think "What do they mean?" is a signal about a central idea.*
B: *Yes, I agree.*

AFTER YOU LISTEN

I THINK CRITICALLY Apply. Work with a partner. Answer the questions. Use the information from the lecture to support your answer.

1. Name two more occupations that you feel would be ideal for each personality type.

2. Which type of personality, a *maximizer* or a *satisficer*, would
   a. probably have a messier home?
   b. be a better leader of an organization?
   c. you want as a parent?

3. Do you think you are more of a *maximizer* or more of a *satisficer*? Explain why.
   A: *I think I'm more of a maximizer.*
   B: *Me, too. I always hate having to make choices.*

J THINK CRITICALLY Interpret a Graph. Work with a partner and discuss these questions.

1. According to the graph, does happiness increase quickly or slowly with a few more choices? Why do you think that is? Does it decrease quickly or slowly with a lot of choices?

2. How are the first and third faces similar? How are they different?

3. Do the ideas in The Happiness Curve support the ideas in *The Paradox of Choice* from the lecture? Explain your answer.

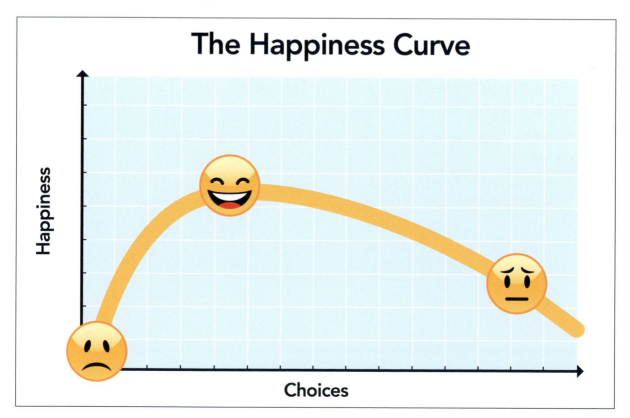

SPEAKING

SPEAKING SKILL **Use Signposts to Organize Ideas**

When speakers want to make several points, they often use *signposts*, or signal words or phrases, to introduce each new point. Using signposts can help you organize your ideas and make it easier for listeners to follow your presentation.

Too many choices create problems for people. **First**, . . .

You can help improve this situation in a few easy ways. **First of all**, . . .

Here are some common signposts:

First . . .	Second . . .	Third . . .
First of all . . .	Secondly . . .	Finally . . .
	Next . . .	Last . . .

K 🎧 **2.22** Listen to segment 3 of the lecture. The professor talks about steps you can take if you are a maximizer. Complete the steps.

SIGNPOST	POINT
1. First,	just _____.
2. Second,	understand that this quality can _____ _____.
3. Last,	do something to _____ _____.

L Work with a partner. What sort of job do you want in the future? Explain your answer to your partner using signposts.

    A: *I want to be a doctor.*

    B: *Really? Why?*

    A: *Lot of reasons. First of all, it's a good, long-term career. Second,...*

PRONUNCIATION SKILL   **Intonation in *Yes/No* and Choice Questions**

Intonation is the way the voice rises and falls when speaking. It is the "music" of language. In *yes/no* questions, the speaker expects a *yes* or *no* answer. In *yes/no* questions, the intonation usually rises at the end. Listen to the examples:

🎧 **2.23**

Would you like coffee?

Are you happier with more choices?

Some questions offer choices. These have a different intonation pattern. Intonation rises on all of the choices except the last one. It falls on the last one:

🎧 **2.24**

Would you like coffee or tea?

M 🎧 **2.25** Listen to the excerpts below. As you listen, draw an arrow at the end of each question to indicate a rising or falling intonation.

1. *"Luz, do you have a question?"*

2. *"Aren't more choices always better?"*

3. *"Would you prefer this menu or this one?"*

4. *"Yuichi, do you think more choices are better?"*

5. *"So, did you buy one?"*

N Work with a partner. Take turns saying the questions in exercise M. Use the correct intonation.

A fabric shop in Kathmandu, Nepal, selling cloth of every color

O Take the quiz. Choose your answer to each question. Then calculate the points to determine your personality.

QUIZ

Are You a *Maximizer* or a *Satisficer?*

1 I often change TV channels looking for something better to watch.   Yes No

2 I often find it difficult deciding which movie to watch.   Yes No

3 I often find it difficult choosing gifts for my friends.   Yes No

4 It is difficult for me to find clothes that I like.   Yes No

5 I need to write several drafts of an email before sending it.   Yes No

6 I often think about different ways of living my life.   Yes No

7 I take a long time doing my homework because I want it to be perfect.   Yes No

8 I am afraid to speak English because I'm not sure of the grammar.   Yes No

KEY: Yes = 2 points   No = 1 point

PERSONALITY TYPE	POINTS
Extreme *Satisficer*	6 points
Satisficer	7–9
A little of both	10–12
Maximizer	13–15
Extreme *Maximizer*	16 points

P **THINK CRITICALLY** **Interpret Results.** Work in small groups. Discuss these questions.

1. Find out about other people in your group. Ask your classmates if they are *maximizers* or *satisficers*. Use correct intonation.

2. Do you think the quiz was accurate? Give some examples to explain your answer.

Less stuff,
more happiness

❝ I'm here to suggest . . .
that less might actually
equal more. **❞**

BEFORE YOU WATCH

A Read the title and information about the TED speaker. *Edit* usually means improving
a piece of writing by fixing problems it may have. What do you think it might mean
to *edit* your life?

GRAHAM HILL   Writer and designer

Graham Hill is an entrepreneur who studied architecture and design. In 2004, he
founded TreeHugger.com, a Web site that promotes a lifestyle that is good for
people as well as the planet. He's currently the CEO of LifeEdited, a project that
shows people how to live well with less.

Graham Hill's idea worth spreading is that we can still be happy with fewer
things, as long as we are able to "edit" our lives in smart, practical ways.

B Read the following statements. Write *A* if you *agree* or *D* if you *disagree*. Then
discuss your answers with a partner.

1. _____ It is a good idea to completely stop buying things.

2. _____ Having less space makes life more difficult.

3. _____ We don't really need most of the things that we own.

VOCABULARY

c 🎧 **2.26** The sentences below will help you learn words in the TED Talk. Read and listen to the sentences. Guess the meanings of the words in bold. Then complete each question with the correct word. Use the correct form of the word.

a. This appliance saves space because it **combines** the functions of a microwave and traditional oven.

b. Only pack what you will need during the trip. Don't include any **extraneous** items.

c. To make more space in my room, I'm going to **digitize** my CDs and photos.

d. I got a loan for my large and expensive house. I lost my job, so now I'm worried about repaying this **debt**.

e. My closet is so full. I have too much **stuff**.

f. This space is **multifunctional**. I use it as a garage and a music studio.

g. The **majority** of Americans—about 60 percent—own their own homes.

h. Coincidentally, I got a job offer on the same day that I found my apartment.

i. If you live in a small apartment, you have to think about space **efficiency**.

j. My new apartment does not have a lot of **storage** space, so I left a lot of my books at my parents' house.

1. When you listen to a lecture, are you sometimes overwhelmed by all of the
_____ information?

2. Many people in the United States have a lot of _____ from buying houses, cars, or from college loans. Is this true in your country?

3. If you _____ all of your expenses (e.g., rent, food, etc.), do they equal more than your income? How could you reduce your expenses?

4. Do you have any _____ furniture in your home? Describe their different uses.

5. Does your home have enough closets and other _____ space for all of your things? What do you do if there is no more space?

6. Mario is going to _____ his photos. This will save a lot of space in his small apartment. What can you put on your computer or online to save space?

7. Have you and a friend ever _____ bought the same thing or worn the same thing on the same day?

8. A dishwasher that fits inside a drawer saves a lot of space. What other products can improve space _____ in a kitchen?

9. Do the _____ of people in your city live in apartments or houses? Has this changed in the last 30 years?

10. How much _____ do you have in your bag? Can you find things easily?

D COMMUNICATE Work in small groups. Take turns answering the questions in exercise C.

A: *What's your answer to question 1?*
B: *Well, I try to keep good notes in class so I don't get overwhelmed.*

WATCH

E ▶ **1.31** **WATCH FOR MAIN IDEAS** Read the statements. Then watch the edited TED Talk by Graham Hill. Write *A* if you think Hill would *agree* or *D* if you think he would *disagree* with each statement. Then discuss your answers with a partner.

1. _____ It is a good idea to stop buying things.

2. _____ Having less space makes life more difficult.

3. _____ We don't really need most of the things that we own.

F THINK CRITICALLY Reflect. Work with a partner. Tell your partner whether you still agree with the same statements in exercise B on page 133. Did your ideas change? Explain why, or why not.

learn**more** 1 in 10 Americans has off-site personal storage. Total personal storage space in the U.S. is 2.3 billion square feet—about three times the size of Manhattan in New York.

WORDS IN THE TALK

environmental footprint (n): the effect that a person, business, or activity has on the health of the planet
flat line (v): to remain the same; not increase

When you take notes, it sometimes helps to record information in a list format. Listen for cues that a speaker is going to list information. Here are some cues to listen for:

Rhetorical questions

Where does this lead?

Numbers

Three challenges/solutions/approaches are . . .

Signposts

First, you can increase efficiency.

Secondly, you can edit your stuff.

In your notes, use a heading and numbers, letters, or bullets to show the information clearly.

G ▶ **1.32** **WATCH FOR DETAILS** Watch each segment of Hill's talk again and complete the notes. More than one answer may be correct.

Segment 1

Too much stuff leads to three problems

1. lots of _____

2. a huge _____

3. _____ levels flat-lined

Segment 2

Less stuff and less space =

1. a smaller _____

2. a great way to _____

3. _____ in your life

Segment 3

Three approaches to live "little"

1. you have to _____ ruthlessly

2. we want _____ efficiency

3. we want _____ and housewares

H ▶ **1.33** **EXPAND YOUR VOCABULARY** Watch the excerpts from the TED Talk. Guess the meanings of the phrases in the box.

let it go	vast majority	by all means
I bet (that)	take a second	make room for

I **WATCH MORE** Go to TED.com to watch the full TED Talk by Graham Hill.

AFTER YOU WATCH

J **THINK CRITICALLY** **Infer.** Work with a small group. Discuss these questions.

1. Hill says, "*We've got to clear the arteries of our lives.*" The word *artery* is usually used in a very different context. Explain how it is usually used and why Hill uses it here.

2. Hill suggests, "*Less stuff and less space are going to equal a smaller footprint.*" How could changes in lifestyle and behavior lead to a smaller environmental footprint?

K **COMMUNICATE** Work with a partner. Discuss your answers to these questions.

A: *One way I'd edit my life is to clear out my closet.*
B: *I hear you! I have way too many clothes that I never wear.*

1. What might be your answer to the question "What's in your box?"

2. What is one way you might "edit" your life?

3. Think about Hill's small apartment. Would you be able to "edit" your life in the same way that he did? Why, or why not?

A "tiny house" in Richmond, Virginia

L **THINK CRITICALLY** **Interpret an Infographic.** Work with a partner. Look at the infographic below. Discuss these questions.

1. Which country has the highest HPI? Which country has the lowest HPI?

2. What do you think people consider when they rate their quality of life?

3. Do any of the HPI results surprise you? Explain your answer.

4. In what ways do you think the HPI relates to the idea of *less is more*?

A Happy Planet?

The Happy Planet Index (HPI) measures the degree to which people in each country live long, happy, sustainable lives.

It is a combination of three measures: 1. longevity: the average age they are likely to live
2. happiness: the quality of life they report on a scale of 1–10
3. sustainability: their environmental footprint

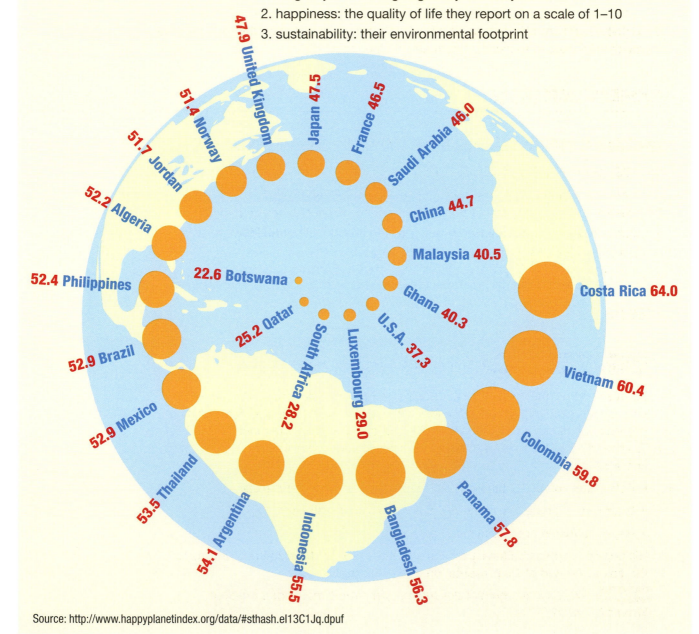

Source: http://www.happyplanetindex.org/data/#sthash.el13C1Jq.dpuf

Put It Together

A **THINK CRITICALLY** **Synthesize.** Work in small groups to complete the chart with information from the lecture in Part 1 and Hill's TED Talk in Part 2.

	PART 1 LECTURE	PART 2 TED TALK
1. What ideas do the lecture and the TED Talk have in common?	too many _choices_ don't increase _____	too much _____ doesn't increase _____
2. What kinds of problems does this cause?		

B **THINK CRITICALLY** **Reflect.** Work with a partner. How do you think having "too much stuff" relates to having "too many choices"?

COMMUNICATE

ASSIGNMENT: Give a Group Presentation

You are going to give a group presentation about the topic "less is more." Your presentation will address the question: Is having lots of choices or a lot of stuff always a good thing? Review the ideas in Parts 1 and 2 and the listening and speaking skills as you prepare your presentation.

PREPARE

PRESENTATION SKILL Connect the Ending to the Beginning

Speakers sometimes end a presentation by referring back to something they said at the beginning. Creating these "bookends" gives a clear structure to your presentation. It can also emphasize an important idea in an interesting way. Try one of these techniques to help you connect your presentation's beginning and ending.

• Ask a question at the beginning of the talk and answer it at the end.

• Start a story at the beginning of a talk and finish it at the end.

• Repeat a theme at the beginning and end of a talk.

Hill begins his presentation by talking about the box on the stage and returns to the box at the end of his presentation. Watch it again.

▶ **1.34** *"What's in the box? It doesn't really matter. I know I don't need it. What's in yours?"*

C Work in small groups. Choose one of the topics below, or think of other ideas. Then answer the questions below about your topic.

☐ It is very easy to get credit (borrow money).

☐ Your idea: _____

☐ There are so many classes and majors to choose from.

☐ Your idea: _____

☐ Big stores and online sites make it possible to buy a lot of stuff for less money.

☐ Your idea: _____

QUESTIONS	YOUR NOTES
1. What are the benefits of this?	
2. Why is this a problem? What impact does it have?	
3. What are some possible solutions?	

D **COLLABORATE** Include the following parts in your presentation. Decide who will present each part.

- **Introduction:** What is the first "bookend?" Will you
  - begin a story
  - ask a question
  - make a bold statement (e.g., Money cannot buy happiness.)

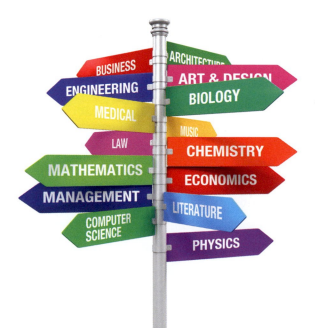

- **Your topic:** Briefly describe your topic.
- **Impact:** Explain the benefits and problems that this situation causes. Consider using signposts to organize your ideas.
- **Solutions:** Give possible solutions.
- **Conclusion:** What will your second bookend be?

E Read the rubric on page 182 before you present. Notice how your presentation will be evaluated. Keep these categories in mind as you present and watch your classmates' presentations.

PRESENT

F Give your presentation to a small group. Watch your classmates' presentations. After you watch each one, provide feedback using the rubric as a guide. Add notes or any other feedback you want to share.

G **THINK CRITICALLY Evaluate.** As a class, discuss what each presenter did well and what might make each presentation even stronger. Decide which two things you did well and which two areas need improvement.

REFLECT

Reflect on what you have learned. Check [✓] your progress.

I can
- ☐ listen for rhetorical questions.
- ☐ use signposts to organize my ideas.
- ☐ use intonation in *yes/no* and choice questions.
- ☐ record information in a list.
- ☐ connect the ending to the beginning in a presentation.

I understand the meaning of these words and can use them.
Circle those you know. Underline those you need to work on.

appreciate AWL	debt	extraneous	option AWL	research AWL
aware of AWL	digitize	impact AWL	overwhelming	satisfied
coincidentally	efficiency	majority AWL	perfectionist	storage
combine	evidence AWL	multifunctional	psychologist AWL	stuff

Justice in the Jungle

A leopard at a man-made watering hole overlooking
Mumbai in the Sanjay Gandhi National Park, India

THINK AND DISCUSS

1 Study the photo and read the caption. What kinds of threats do you think leopards face from human beings?

2 Read the title of this unit. What do you think this unit will be about?

Juliana Machado Ferreira: Fighting the Traffickers

BEFORE YOU LISTEN

A COMMUNICATE Work with a partner. Discuss these questions.

1. Do you, or does someone you know, have a pet? What kind of animal is it?

2. Where do people usually get their pets?

3. Would you like to have a wild animal as a pet? Why, or why not?

B THINK CRITICALLY Predict. Look at the photos and read the caption. You're going to hear an interview with Juliana Machado Ferreira. What do you think she does to fight wildlife trafficking? Discuss with a partner.

National Geographic Explorer Juliana Machado Ferreira at work in the forests of Brazil and in her lab (inset). Ferreira is a conservation biologist fighting illegal wildlife trafficking — the buying and selling of protected wild animals.

VOCABULARY

C 🎧 **2.27** Read and listen to the sentences with words from the interview. Guess the meaning of each word in bold. Then complete each question or sentence below with the correct word. Use the correct form of the word.

a. Protecting wildlife is **crucial.** If we do not, some animals will disappear forever.

b. The effect of trafficking on some tropical birds has been **devastating.** There are only a few of these birds left today.

c. Some species of birds look very similar, so it is difficult to **detect** differences between them.

d. This new technology has the **potential** to find traffickers; however, it has not been fully tested yet.

e. The police **seized** a truck that was carrying hundreds of wild birds. They arrested the driver and took the birds away.

f. Buying and selling most wild animals is **illegal.** If the police catch you, you may go to jail.

g. Scientists and government officials are working together to **maintain** biodiversity—the number and variety of species that live in the country.

h. Governments should work together to **combat** climate change before it's too late.

i. Many species of animals, such as orangutans, are disappearing because humans have destroyed their **habitat.** Now they have nowhere to live.

j. Wildlife trafficking continues because **consumers** want these animals for pets.

1. In most countries, buying and selling drugs is a(n) _____ activity. What are some others?

2. People love their pets so much that they often spend a lot of money on them. What pet products are the most popular with _____ in your country?

3. Too much rain or too little rain can both be _____ for a country. What are the consequences of each, and which do you think is worse?

4. Governments can do a lot to protect wild animals and to _____ trafficking, but experts say that ordinary people also play a _____ role. What do you think ordinary people can do to help?

5. The police are using new techniques to _____ traffickers. They can monitor traffickers' movement even when they are deep in the jungle.

6. The government announced that it will _____ any wild animals that they find in markets and return the animals to their original _____ .

7. The goal of the new law is to _____ the current bird population. It may even have the _____ to help the population to return to the level of 10 years ago.

D **COMMUNICATE** Work in a small group. Take turns answering questions 1–4 in exercise C.

LISTEN

> **LISTENING SKILL** **Listen for Phrases That Signal What to Expect**
>
> Speakers often give their listeners signals about what to expect next. Listening for these signals will help you predict what the speaker is going to say. It will also help you follow and understand what the speaker is talking about.
>
> **To signal a list**
>
> *There are many/several/three . . . types of/kinds of/ways . . .*
>
> *There are many kinds of trafficking.*
>
> **To signal a consequence or result**
>
> *If . . . , (then) . . .*
>
> *If trafficking does not end, . . .*
>
> **To signal additional examples or ideas**
>
> *Besides . . .*
>
> *Not only do . . . but also . . .*
>
> *Not only does this help fight trafficking, but it can also . . .*

E Read the excerpts from the interview with Ferreira. Then choose what information you expect to hear next. Use the signal words in bold to help you.

1. *"There are **several different kinds of** trafficking . . ."*

   a. a definition of trafficking

   b. a list of types of trafficking

   c. an explanation of the consequences of trafficking

2. *"**If** the current level of wildlife trafficking continues, . . ."*

   a. a possible end result of this situation

   b. the steps in this process

   c. an explanation of why trafficking is so harmful

3. *"The disappearance of these species has consequences **not only** for entire ecosystems . . ."*

   a. other species that may also disappear

   b. the ways in which entire ecosystems may change

   c. other ways in which the disappearance of species will have an impact

WORDS IN THE INTERVIEW

genetic marker (n): a piece of DNA that is in a known location so it can be used to study the species

4. *"**If** the animals from one region are released in a different environment, . . ."*

    a. a good reason to release the animals

    b. a place where the animals could be released

    c. a consequence of releasing the animals

F   **2.28**   **1.35**   **LISTEN FOR MAIN IDEAS** Listen to the interview. Then check [✓] the three statements that you think Ferreira would agree with.

1. _____ Trafficking live animals happens because consumers want to buy them.

2. _____ New scientific advances can help maintain and protect bird populations.

3. _____ It is crucial to help animals adapt to their habitats.

4. _____ Trafficking harms animal populations and may lead to their extinction.

5. _____ People can better protect these animals by caring for them as pets.

G   **2.29**   **LISTEN FOR DETAILS** Listen to segment 1 of the interview. Complete the outline below about different forms of trafficking.

Wildlife Trafficking in Brazil: Three Main Kinds

I.   body parts:

    • for souvenirs, _____ accessories, cosmetics, and _____
                            1   2

II.   zoos and _____ collectors
                       3

III.   live wild animals for _____:
                                 4

    • government not sure exact figure; seized > _____ live animals just in
                                                     5

    São Paulo in _____
                        6

    • _____ = most popular; hundreds of thousands sold annually
                  7

    in street _____
                       8

    • if this continues, some species → _____
                                               9

    • consequences for ecosystems as well as _____ quality of life
                                                                  10

Captive and critically endangered
Lear's macaw, São Paulo, Brazil

H 🎧 **2.30** **LISTEN FOR DETAILS** Listen to segment 2 of the interview. Read the sentences below and write *T* for *true*, *F* for *false*, or *N* if there is not enough information to decide.

1. _____ One reason that it is difficult to solve the problem of wildlife trafficking in Brazil is the country's size.

2. _____ Birds in the north of the country have adapted to a hot, wet climate, and birds in the south have adapted to a cooler climate.

3. _____ Animals from one region of the country might not survive if they are released in a different environment.

4. _____ The police have used genetic markers to find the birds' habitat.

5. _____ Ferreira has collected information on all of the birds' genetic markers.

AFTER YOU LISTEN

I **THINK CRITICALLY** **Infer.** Read the questions below. Choose the answer for each question. Then compare your answers with a partner.

1. According to the interview, which of the following might be uses of illegally traded wild animals?
   a. museum exhibits   **b.** jewelry   **c.** food

2. What is the size of the wild-bird trafficking market in Brazil?
   a. 30,000 birds   **b.** 1 million birds   **c.** no one knows for sure

3. What do the police do when they seize birds far away from their habitat?
   a. They release the birds.
   b. They find genetic markers.
   c. They try to discover where the birds come from.

4. Can scientists tell where these birds come from?
   a. Yes, they can use genetic markers to determine their original habitat.
   b. Not yet. Scientists are developing tools but they are not ready to use.
   c. No, there is no way to discover their original habitat.

5. Ferreira is a scientist. Why does she do interviews like this one?
   a. She hopes to educate the public.
   b. She hopes to change her country's laws.
   c. She hopes to get other scientists interested in her work.

J **THINK CRITICALLY** **Interpret an Infographic.** Work with a small group. The infographic below shows facts about the exotic pet trade in the U.S. Study the infographic and then discuss these questions.

1. Why do you think big cats (e.g. tigers and lions) and primates (e.g. monkeys) are such popular pets?

2. Why do you think so many wild animals in the pet trade die so quickly?

3. Does anything surprise you about this infographic? Explain your answer.

The Truth Behind the Exotic Pet Trade

The exotic pet trade is worth $15 billion in the U.S. alone

There are an estimated 5000–7000 tigers in the U.S. alone, more than there are left in the wild.

Captive 5000　**Wild 3200**

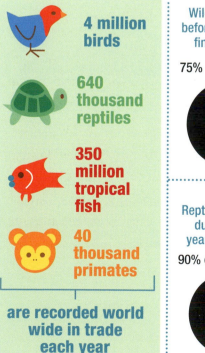

2000 of them live in Texas, which is the 2nd largest tiger population in the world.

U.S. Exotic Pet Laws

● Bans most dangerous wild animals as pets (big cats, bears, wolves, primates, some reptiles).

● Bans some species of dangerous wild animals as pets but allows others.

● Does not ban dangerous wild animals as pets but requires permits for some species.

● Does not regulate or restrict dangerous wild animals at all.

It's estimated that between **10-20,000 big cats** are currently in private hands in the United States.

15,000 primates are also believed to live in U.S. homes, from chimpanzees to capuchins to lemurs to marmosets.

Snakes are the most common "pet" reptile—about 3% of U.S. households own **7.3 million pet reptiles**.

4 million birds

640 thousand reptiles

350 million tropical fish

40 thousand primates

are recorded world wide in trade each year

Wild birds that die before reaching their final destination

75% die　25% survive

Reptile survival rate during the first year of ownership

90% die　10% survive

SPEAKING

Sometimes an interviewee doesn't answer a question completely, and the interviewer may need to ask another question. Or one answer may lead to another question. Questions like these are called *follow-up* questions. Follow-up questions may:

- ask for reasons
- ask for examples
- ask about effects or consequences
- ask about the next step
- ask for more details or an explanation

K **COMMUNICATE** Work with a partner. An interview is often a series of follow-up questions. Read the interviewer's questions. Write the purpose of each question using the list from the skill box.

1. *"Can you describe the market for wild animals as pets in Brazil? How big is it? Which animals are the most popular?"*

   To ask _____

2. *"What are the consequences of this type of wildlife trafficking?"*

   To ask _____

3. *"What happens to the animals when the police find them?"*

   To ask _____

4. *"Why not? Why is it important to release animals in their original habitat?"*

   To ask _____

5. *"How do you hope your work will help with this problem?"*

   To ask _____

L Work with a small group. Which of the animals in the chart on page 151 are most in danger of extinction? Rank them in order of how much danger you think they are in (1 = great danger, 4 = least danger).

   A: *I think the Black Rhino is in great danger.*

   B: *I agree. I read that there are only a few hundred left.*

   A: *Let's rank that as 1.*

Endangered animals and their habitats

_____ **African Elephant**
Subtropical forests
and grasslands
in central Africa

_____ **Polar Bear**
Arctic

_____ **Chimpanzee**
Forests in central Africa

_____ **Sumatran
Orangutan**
Tropical forests
in Indonesia

_____ **Great White
Shark**
Pacific and Indian Oceans

_____ **Bald Eagle**
Forests near lakes
in North America

_____ **Black Rhinoceros**
Sub-tropical grasslands
in southern Africa

_____ **Giant Panda**
Temperate forests
in China

_____ **Bluefin Tuna**
Atlantic and Pacific Oceans

_____ **Gray Whale**
Atlantic, Pacific, and
Arctic Oceans

M CRITICAL THINKING Reflect. Work with a partner. Discuss the reasons why the animals in exercise L are in danger. Which of the factors below do you think have had an impact on them? Then look at the answers on page 161. Do any of the answers surprise you?

1. trafficking in live animals

2. illegal hunting or fishing

3. poaching for animal body parts

4. loss of habitat because of climate change

5. loss of habitat because humans have taken habitats

6. pollution

N 🎧 2.33 Listen to these excerpts from the interview and read along. Draw ➚ when you hear a rising intonation, and ➘ when you hear a falling intonation.

1. *Can you describe the market for wild animals as pets in Brazil? How big is it?*

2. *Which animals are the most popular?*

3. *Why not? Why is it important to release animals in their original habitat?*

O 🎧 2.34 Work with a partner. Take turns repeating the interviewer's questions with correct intonation.

1. *What is wildlife trafficking?*

2. *What are the consequences of this type of wildlife trafficking?*

3. *What happens to the animals when the police find them?*

4. *Why not? Why is it important to release animals in their original habitat?*

5. *What message do you want to get out to the public about this issue?*

P COLLABORATE Work with a small group. Imagine you could meet Ferreira. What follow-up questions would you like to ask her? Use appropriate intonation in *Wh-* questions.

A: *Are you still working on the genetic marker project?*
B: *Yes, I am.*
A: *What kind of progress have you made on the project?*

A drone's-eye view of conservation

❝ Drones have tremendous potential. ❞

BEFORE YOU WATCH

A Work with a partner. Read the title of the talk and the information about the TED speaker. How do you think a drone can help with wildlife conservation?

A: *The drones might be able to help police find poachers.*

B: *How do you think the drones will find poachers?*

LIAN PIN KOH   Drones Ecologist

Lian Pin Koh is an environmental scientist; he also loves to invent things. He started ConservationDrones.org, which uses *drones*—low-cost unmanned flying machines—to help with wildlife conservation. Koh says he got the idea for his drone project after he went on a long walk through the jungle carrying heavy equipment. He thought, "There has to be a better way to do this!"

Koh's idea worth spreading is that drones can be an incredibly effective and affordable way to help protect the world's wildlife.

VOCABULARY

B 🎧 **2.35** The sentences below will help you learn words in the TED Talk. Read and listen to the sentences. Guess the meanings of the words in bold. Then match each word to its definition.

a. Hidden cameras can **capture** images of the animals in their natural habitat.

b. The habitats of many wild animals are **contracting** because humans need more living space.

c. The **objective** of the new law is to reduce wildlife trafficking.

d. Conservationists in Nepal have **acquired** a drone. It is a new model, so they will test it before they fly it over the jungle.

e. New technology has made it easier to **monitor** wildlife populations from far away.

f. Some of the rarest species live in **remote** areas of the jungle where it is hard to reach them.

g. Poaching—the illegal hunting of wild animals—is one of the biggest **threats** to larger animals such as rhinos.

h. Scientists plan to **survey** the elephant population of the entire continent. They will publish the results next year.

i. It is easier to find money for the protection of animals that are considered attractive, such as panda bears and chimpanzees, than for animals that may be less **appealing,** such as fish and frogs.

j. The camera on the drone focuses **automatically.** The scientists do not need to control it.

1. _____ (adj) attractive

2. _____ (v) examine an entire situation

3. _____ (adj) far away

4. _____ (v) becoming smaller

5. _____ (adv) by itself; independently

6. _____ (n) dangers

7. _____ (v) gotten

8. _____ (v) record an image or sound

9. _____ (n) goal

10. _____ (v) watch and check on

C **COMMUNICATE** Work with a partner. Take turns answering the following questions. Use the items in bold in your answers.

> A: *What do you think is the biggest threat to wildlife?*
>
> B: *I think climate change is a the biggest threat.*

1. What do you think is the biggest **threat** to wildlife?

2. Why do you think some people want to **acquire** wild animals as pets? Are they more **appealing** than other animals? Explain your answer.

3. What is the most **remote** area that you have ever visited? Describe it to your partner.

4. Some experts hope to completely stop all poaching and trafficking. Do you think this is a realistic **objective?** Explain why, or why not.

WATCH

D ▶ **1.36** **LISTEN FOR SIGNALS** Read the excerpts from the talk. Complete each statement. Use the signal words in bold to help you. Then watch segment 1 of the talk to check your answers.

1. *"Nepal is always looking for **new ways** to help with protecting the forests and wildlife …"*

   I expect to hear about

   a. a report on Nepal's successful fight against traffickers.

   b. additional help to fight wildlife trafficking.

   c. a surprising fact about wildlife trafficking.

2. *"**Not only** does the drone **give you** a bird's-eye view of the landscape, **but** it **also** …"*

   I expect to hear about

   a. how a drone is like a bird.

   b. a result of using a drone.

   c. another use of a drone.

3. *"We believe that drones have **tremendous potential, not only for** combating wildlife crime, **but also …**"*

   I expect to hear about

   a. additional purposes for drones.

   b. an explanation of how drones fight wildlife trafficking.

   c. a list of other ways to fight wildlife trafficking.

WORDS IN THE TALK
algorithms (n): instructions for solving a problem
deforestation (n): the destruction of trees
logging (n): the cutting down of trees in order to sell the wood
plantations (n): large farms
prototype (n): first model of something

E ▶ **1.37** **WATCH FOR MAIN IDEAS** Watch the edited TED Talk. Then check the statement that best expresses the speaker's main idea.

1. _____ The military is effective at stopping poaching and wildlife trafficking.

2. _____ Drones can improve wildlife conservation efforts.

3. _____ Drones are best used to stop poachers and wildlife trackers.

4. _____ Deforestation is causing many animals to lose their habitats.

5. _____ Wildlife conservationists can use a drone to stop poachers and traffickers.

NOTE-TAKING SKILL **Use Mind Maps**

Sometimes it is useful to take notes in a freer way than with lists and outlines. Mind maps are a flexible approach that help you visualize the relationships among the ideas in your notes. Mind maps usually begin with a central concept. You can add and connect ideas as you listen, or later, when you review your notes.

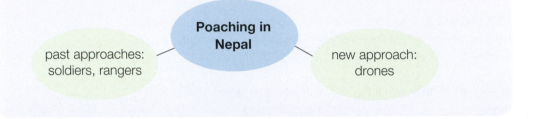

past approaches: soldiers, rangers — **Poaching in Nepal** — new approach: drones

An elephant photographed by a drone

F ▶ **1.38** **WATCH FOR DETAILS** Watch segment 2 of the talk. While you watch, take notes using a mind map. Compare your answers with a partner's.

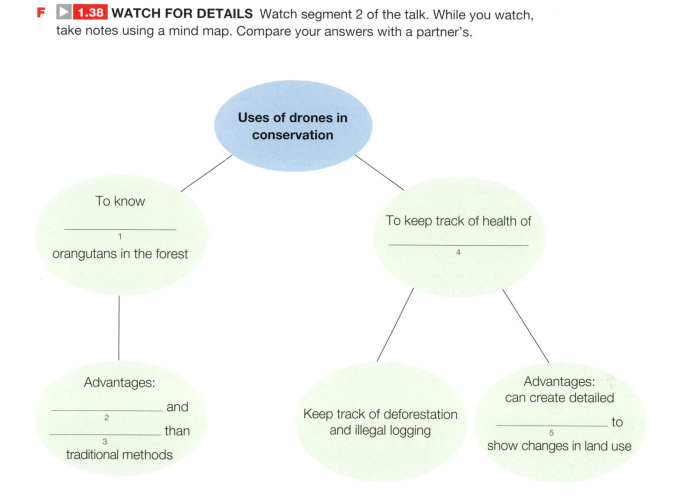

G **THINK CRITICALLY** **Reflect.** Work with a small group. Discuss these questions.

1. Do you think conservation drones will be more successful than traditional methods in combatting wildlife crime? Why, or why not?

2. What might be some challenges in using conservation drones? Explain your answer.

3. Do you think drones could be useful in Brazil to combat the trafficking of wild animals? Why or why not?

4. Do you know of other conservation issues that drones could help with, either animal or environmental? Explain how they could help.

> under threat   bird's-eye view   keep track of   labor-intensive   breaking out

I **WATCH MORE** Go to TED.com to watch the full TED Talk by Lian Pin Koh.

AFTER YOU WATCH

J **COMMUNICATE** Work in a small group. Koh thinks there are other potential uses
for conservation drones. Look at the graphic below and read the captions. Then
discuss these questions.

1. What do you think the benefits might be for wildlife conservationists for each
   new use?

2. Which future use do you think might be the most useful in maintaining and
   protecting wildlife and their habitats?

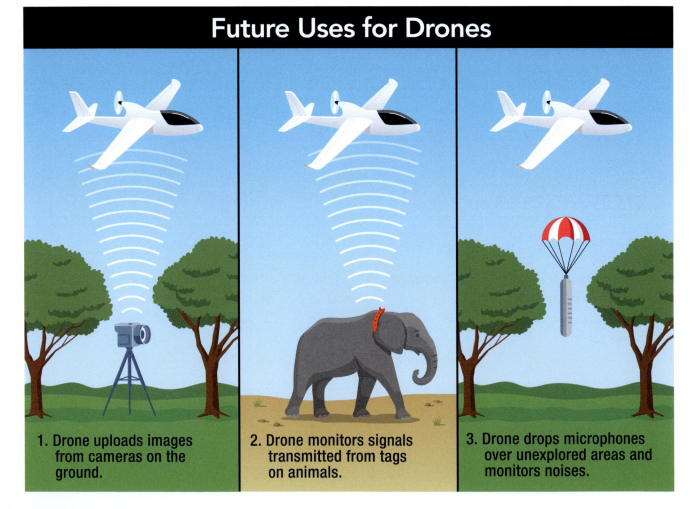

Future Uses for Drones

1. Drone uploads images from cameras on the ground.

2. Drone monitors signals transmitted from tags on animals.

3. Drone drops microphones over unexplored areas and monitors noises.

Put It Together

A **THINK CRITICALLY** **Synthesize.** Work in a small group. Think about all of the different threats to wildlife and natural habitats that you have learned about in this unit. Organize these threats in the table below.

THREATS TO WILDLIFE	
ILLEGAL ACTIVITIES	**HABITAT LOSS/CHANGE**
Wildlife trafficking	Animal extinction

B **THINK CRITICALLY** **Apply.** Work in a small group. What are some ways in which people might contribute to the threats to wildlife and natural habitats without realizing it? Are there any ways in which our actions and decisions could reduce those threats? Explain your answers.

    A: *Juliana Machado Ferreira said cosmetics can be made from animals.*

    B: *Right. People might buy them without knowing that. We should read cosmetic labels carefully to avoid this.*

COMMUNICATE

ASSIGNMENT: Give a Group Presentation You and your group will prepare and give a presentation with visuals about an animal that is under threat. Review the ideas in Parts 1 and 2 and the listening and speaking skills as you prepare your presentation.

PRESENTATION SKILL Use Visuals Effectively

Good presentations use visual support—such as photographs, infographics, or presentation slides—effectively. These visuals can sometimes convey ideas more effectively and quickly than words.

Think about the following when choosing visuals for your presentation:

- Choose visuals that help the audience understand your point and visualize what you are describing.

- Keep your visuals clear and simple—remember that some of your audience will be sitting far away from you.

- Connect your visual clearly to the content of the presentation.

- If you use words on your visual, use short simple phrases and don't read them.

- Limit the number of visuals you use to the most impactful ones.

- Don't turn away from your audience to look at your visual.

C **THINK CRITICALLY** **Reflect.** What different types of visuals did Koh use in his TED Talk? Which do you think were the most effective? Explain why.

D Work in a small group. Prepare your presentation and visuals. Follow the steps below.

1. Decide which animal your group would like to present on. You can use information about an animal from this unit or your own ideas. Include the following information about the animal:

- Where does it typically live?

- What is its habitat like?

- Is it an endangered animal? (How serious is the threat? How many are left?)

- What kinds of threats does it face?

- How are conservationists dealing with these threats?

2. In your group, decide who will take the following roles:

- Find at least one visual that supports your presentation.

- Describe the animal, its habitat, and its current situation.

- Explain the threat(s) facing the animal.

- Explain how these threats are being addressed.

E Read the rubric on page 182 before you present. Notice how your presentation will be evaluated. Keep these categories in mind as you present and watch your classmates' presentations.

PRESENT

F Give your presentation to the class. Watch your classmates' presentations. After you watch each one, provide feedback using the rubric as a guide. Add notes or any other feedback you want to share.

G **THINK CRITICALLY** **Evaluate.** In your group, discuss the feedback you received. As a class, discuss what each group did well and what might make each presentation even stronger.

REFLECT

Reflect on what you have learned. Check [✓] your progress.

I can
- [ ] recognize phrases that signal what to expect.
- [ ] ask follow-up questions.
- [ ] use intonation in *Wh-* questions.
- [ ] use mind maps in my note taking.
- [ ] use visuals effectively in a presentation.

I understand the meaning of these words and can use them.
Circle those you know. Underline those you need to work on.

acquire AWL	consumer AWL	habitat	potential AWL
appealing	contract AWL	illegal AWL	remote
automatically AWL	crucial AWL	maintain AWL	seize
capture	detect AWL	monitor AWL	survey AWL
combat	devastating	objective AWL	threat

Answers for Exercise M, page 151:

Rhino (2,3,5)	Tuna (2)	Chimpanzee (1,2,5)	Elephant (3,5)	Whale (5)
Orangutan (1,5)	Panda (2,5)	Polar Bear (4,5)	Shark (2,3)	Eagle (5)

Independent Student Handbook

The *Independent Student Handbook* is a resource you can use during and after this course. It provides additional support for listening, speaking, note-taking, pronunciation, presentation, and vocabulary skills.

Listening Strategies

Predicting

Speakers giving formal talks usually begin by introducing themselves and then introducing their topic. Listen carefully to the introduction of the topic, and try to anticipate what you will hear.

Strategies:

- Use visual information including titles on the board, on slides, or in a PowerPoint presentation.
- Think about what you already know about the topic.
- Ask yourself questions that you think the speaker might answer.
- Listen for specific introduction phrases.

Listening for Main Ideas

It is important to be able to tell the difference between a speaker's main ideas and supporting details. In college, professors will often test students' understanding of the main ideas more than of specific details.

Strategies:

- Listen carefully to the introduction. The main idea is often stated at the end of the introduction.
- Listen for rhetorical questions, or questions that the speaker asks and then answers. Often the answer is the statement of the main idea.
- Notice ideas that are repeated or rephrased. Repetition and rephrasing often signal main ideas (see Common Phrases for Presenting, Repeating and Rephrasing, page 166).

Listening for Details (Examples)

A speaker will often provide examples that support a main idea. A good example can help you understand and remember the main idea better.

Strategies:

- Listen for specific phrases that introduce an example (see Common Phrases for Presenting, Giving Examples, page 166).
- Notice if an example comes after a general statement from the speaker or is leading into a general statement.
- If there are several examples, decide if they all support the same idea.

Listening for Details (Reasons)

Speakers often give reasons or list causes and/or effects to support their ideas.

Strategies:

- Notice nouns that might signal causes/reasons (e.g., *factors, influences, causes, reasons*) or effects/results (e.g., *effects, results, outcomes, consequences*).
- Notice verbs that might signal causes/reasons (e.g., *contribute to, affect, influence, determine, produce, result in*) or effects/results (often these are passive, e.g., *is affected by*).
- Listen for specific phrases that introduce reasons/causes and effects/results (see Common Phrases for Presenting, Giving Reasons or Causes, page 165).

Understanding the Structure of the Presentation

An organized speaker will use certain expressions to alert you to the important information that will follow. Notice signal words and phrases that tell you how the presentation is organized and the relationship between main ideas.

Introduction

A good introduction includes something like a thesis statement, which identifies the topic and gives an idea of how the lecture or presentation will be organized. Here are some expressions to listen for that indicate a speaker is introducing a topic (see also Common Phrases for Presenting, Introducing a Topic, page 165):

I'll be talking about …	*My topic is …*
There are basically two groups …	*There are three reasons …*

Body

In the body of the lecture, the speaker will usually expand upon the topic. The speaker will use phrases that tell you the order of events or subtopics and their relationship to each other. Here are some expressions to listen for to help follow the body of a lecture (see also Common Phrases for Presenting, Listing or Sequencing, page 165):

The first / next / final (point) is …	*First / Next / Finally, let's look at …*
Another reason is …	*However, …*

Conclusion

In a conclusion, the speaker often summarizes what has already been said and may discuss what it means or make predictions or suggestions. Sometimes speakers ask a question in the conclusion to get the audience to think more about the topic. Here are some expressions to listen for that indicate a speaker is giving a conclusion (see also Common Phrases for Presenting, Conclusion, page 166):

In conclusion, …	*In summary, …*
As you can see …	*To review, + (restatement of main points)*

Understanding Meaning from Context

Speakers may use words that are new to you, or you may not understand exactly what they've said. In these situations, you can guess the meaning of a particular word or fill in the gaps of what you've understood by using the context or situation itself.

Strategies:

- Don't panic. You don't always understand every word of what a speaker says in your first language, either.
- Use context clues to fill in the blanks. What did you understand just before or just after the missing part? What did the speaker probably say?
- Listen for words and phrases that signal a definition or explanation (see Common Phrases for Presenting, Signaling a Definition, page 166).

Recognizing a Speaker's Bias

Speakers often have an opinion about the topic they are discussing. It's important for you to know if they are objective or subjective about the topic. Objective speakers do not express an opinion. Subjective speakers have a bias or strong feeling about the topic.

Strategies:

- Notice words like adjectives, adverbs, and modals that the speaker uses (e.g., *ideal, horribly, should, shouldn't*). These suggest that the speaker has a bias.
- Listen to the speaker's tone. Does he or she sound excited, happy, or bored?
- When presenting another point of view on the topic, is that other point of view given much less time and attention by the speaker?
- Listen for words that signal opinions (see Common Phrases for Classroom Communication, Expressing Opinions, page 167).

Common Phrases for Presenting

The chart below provides some common signposts and signal words and phrases that speakers use in the introduction, body, and conclusion of a presentation.

INTRODUCTION

Introducing a Topic

I'm going to talk about …

My topic is …

I'm going to present …

I plan to discuss …

Let's start with …

Today we're going to talk about …

So we're going to show you …

Now/Right/So/Well, (pause) let's look at …

There are three groups/reasons/effects/factors …

There are four steps in this process.

BODY

Listing or Sequencing

First/First of all/The first (noun)/To start/To begin, …

Second/Secondly/The second/Next/Another/Also/Then/In addition, …

Last/The last/Finally …

There are many/several/three types/kinds of/ways, …

Signaling Problems/Solutions

The one problem/issue/challenge (with) is …

The one solution/answer/response is …

Giving Reasons or Causes

Because + (clause): Because it makes me feel happy …

Because of + (noun phrase): Because of climate change …

Due to + (noun phrase) …

Since + (clause) …

The reason that I like hip-hop is …

One reason that people listen to music is …

One factor is + (noun phrase) …

The main reason that…

Giving Results or Effects

so + (clause): so I went to the symphony

Therefore, + (sentence): Therefore, I went to the symphony.

As a result, + (sentence).

Consequently, + (sentence).

… causes + (noun phrase)

… leads to + (noun phrase)

… had an impact/effect on + (noun phrase)

If … then …

Giving Examples

The first example is…

Here's an example of what I mean …

For instance, …

For example, …

Let me give you an example …

… such as …

… like …

Repeating and Rephrasing

What you need to know is …

I'll say this again, …

So again, let me repeat …

The most important point is …

Signaling Additional Examples or Ideas

Not only … but

Besides …

Not only do … but also

Signaling to Stop Taking Notes

You don't need this for the test.

This information is in your books/on your handout/on the website.

You don't have to write all this down.

Identifying a Side Track

This is off-topic, …

On a different subject, …

As an aside, …

That reminds me ….

Returning to a Previous Topic

Getting back to our previous discussion, …

To return to our earlier topic …

OK, getting back on topic …

So to return to what we were saying, …

Signaling a Definition

Which means …

What that means is …

Or …

In other words, …

Another way to say that is …

That is …

That is to say …

Talking about Visuals

This graph/infographic/diagram shows/explains …

The line/box/image represents …

The main point of this visual is …

You can see …

From this we can see …

CONCLUSION

Concluding

Well/So, that's how I see it.

In conclusion, …

In summary, …

To sum up, …

As you can see, …

At the end, …

To review, + (restatement of main points)

Common Phrases For Classroom Communication

The chart below shows some common phrases for expressing ideas and opinions in class and for interacting with your classmates during pair and group work exercises.

PHRASES FOR EXPRESSING YOURSELF

Expressing Opinions	Expressing Likes and Dislikes
I think …	*I like …*
I believe …	*I prefer …*
I'm sure …	*I love …*
In my opinion/view …	*I can't stand …*
If you ask me, …	*I hate …*
Personally, …	*I really don't like …*
To me, …	*I don't care for …*

Giving Facts	Giving Tips or Suggestions
There is evidence/proof …	Imperatives (e.g., *Try to get more sleep.*)
Experts claim/argue …	*You/We should/shouldn't …*
Studies show …	*You/We ought to …*
Researchers found …	*It's (not) a good idea to …*
The record shows …	*I suggest (that) …*
	Let's …
	How about + (noun/gerund)
	What about + (noun/gerund)
	Why don't we/you …
	You/We could …

PHRASES FOR INTERACTING WITH OTHERS

Agreeing	Clarifying/Checking Your Understanding
I agree.	*So are you saying that … ?*
True.	*So what you mean is … ?*
Good point.	*What do you mean?*
Exactly.	*How's that?*
Absolutely.	*How so?*
I was just about to say that.	*I'm not sure I understand/follow.*
Definitely.	*Do you mean … ?*
Right!	*I'm not sure what you mean.*

PHRASES FOR INTERACTING WITH OTHERS

Disagreeing

I disagree.

I'm not so sure about that.

I don't know.

That's a good point, but I don't agree.

I see what you mean, but I think that …

Checking Others' Understanding

Does that make sense?

Do you understand?

Do you see what I mean?

Is that clear?

Are you following me?

Do you have any questions?

Asking for Opinions

What do you think?

We haven't heard from you in a while.

Do you have anything to add?

What are your thoughts?

How do you feel?

What's your opinion?

Taking Turns

Can I say something?

May I say something?

Could I add something?

Can I just say … ?

May I continue?

Can I finish what I was saying?

Would you finish what you were saying?

Did you finish your thought?

Let me finish.

Let's get back to …

Interrupting Politely

Excuse me.

Pardon me.

Forgive me for interrupting, …

I hate to interrupt, but …

Can I stop you for a second?

Asking for Repetition

Could you say that again?

I'm sorry?

I didn't catch what you said.

I'm sorry. I missed that. What did you say?

Could you repeat that, please?

Showing Interest

I see.

Good for you.

Really?

Seriously?

Um-hmm.

No kidding!

Wow.

And? (Then what?)

That's funny / amazing / incredible / awful!

Note-Taking Strategies

Taking notes is a personalized skill. It is important to develop a notetaking system that works well for you. However, there are some common strategies that you can use to improve your note-taking.

BEFORE YOU LISTEN

Focus Try to clear your mind before the speaker begins so you can pay attention. If possible, review previous notes or what you already know about the topic.

Predict If you know the topic of the talk, think about what you might hear.

LISTEN

Take Notes by Hand

Research suggests that taking notes by hand rather than on a laptop or tablet is more effective. Taking notes by hand requires you to summarize, rephrase, and synthesize the information. This helps you *encode* the information, or put it into a form that you can understand and remember.

Listen for Signal Words and Phrases

Speakers often use signal words and phrases (see page 165) to organize their ideas and indicate what they are going to talk about. Listening for signal words and phrases can help you decide what information to write down in your notes.

Today we're going to talk about three alternative methods that are ecofriendly, fast, and efficient.

Condense (Shorten) Information

- As you listen, focus on the most important ideas. The speaker will usually repeat, define, explain, and/or give examples of these ideas. Take notes on these ideas.

    Speaker: *Worldwide, people are using and wasting huge amounts of plastic. For example, Americans throw away 35 million plastic bottles a year.*

    Notes: *Waste plastic*
    Amer. 35 mil plastic bottles/year

- Don't write full sentences. Write only key words (nouns, verbs, adjectives), phrases, or short sentences.

    Full sentence: *The Maldives built a sea wall around the main island of Male.*

    Notes: *Built sea wall—Male*

- Leave out information that is obvious.

    Full sentence: *Van den Bercken fell in love with the music of Handel.*

    Notes: *VDB loves Handel*

- Write numbers and statistics. (*35 mil; 91%*)
- Use abbreviations (e.g., ft., min., yr) and symbols (=, ≠, >, <, %, →)
- Use indenting. Write main ideas on the left side of the paper. Indent details.

    Benefits of car sharing

    Save $

    Saved $300-400/mo.

- Write details under key terms to help you remember them.

- Write the definitions of important new words from the presentation.

AFTER YOU LISTEN

- Review your notes soon after the lecture or presentation. Add any details you missed and remember.
- Clarify anything you don't understand in your notes with a classmate or teacher.
- Add or highlight main ideas. Cross out details that aren't important or necessary.
- Rewrite anything that is hard to read or understand. Rewrite your notes in an outline or other graphic organizer to organize the information more clearly (see Organizing Information, below).
- Use arrows, boxes, diagrams, or other visual cues to show relationships between ideas.

ORGANIZING INFORMATION

Sometimes it is helpful to take notes using a graphic organizer. You can use one to take notes while you are listening or to organize your notes after you listen. Here are some examples of graphic organizers:

Flowcharts are used to show processes, or cause/effect relationships.

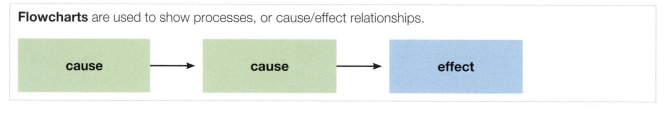

Mind maps show the connection between concepts. The main idea is usually in the center with supporting ideas and details around it.

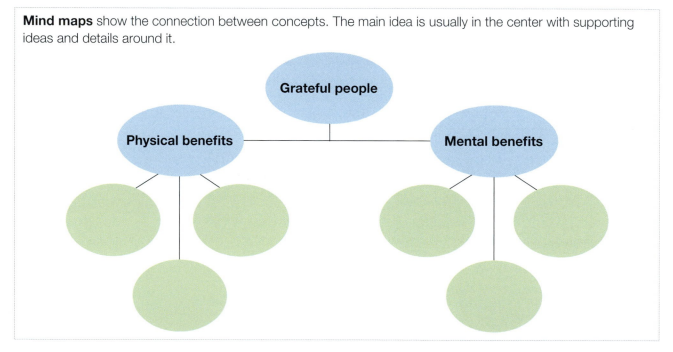

Outlines show the relationship between main ideas and details.

To use an outline for taking notes, write the main ideas starting at the left margin of your paper. Below the main ideas, indent and write the supporting ideas and details. You may do this as you listen, or go back and rewrite your notes as an outline later.

    I. Saving Water

        A. Why is it crucial to save water?

            1. Save money

            2. Not enough fresh water in the world

T-charts compare two topics.

Hands-On Learning	
Advantages	**Disadvantages**
1. Uses all the senses (sight, touch, etc.) 2. Encourages student participation 3. Helps memory	1. Requires many types of materials 2. May be more difficult to manage large classes 3. Requires more teacher time to prepare

---

Timelines show a sequence of events.

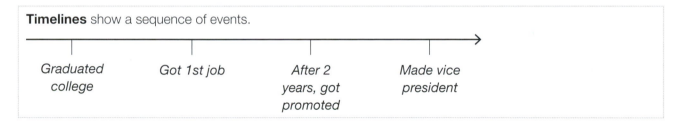

Graduated college   Got 1st job   After 2 years, got promoted   Made vice president

---

Venn diagrams compare and contrast two or more topics. The overlapping areas show similarities.

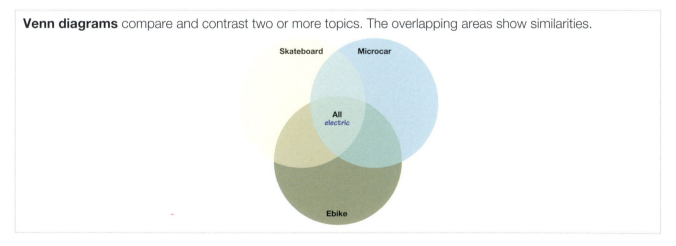

Pronunciation Strategies

When speaking English, it's important to pay attention to the pronunciation of specific sounds. It is also important to learn how to use rhythm, stress, and pausing. The charts below provide some tips about English pronunciation.

SPECIFIC SOUNDS

Vowels			Consonants		
Symbol	Key Word	Pronunciation	Symbol	Key Word	Pronunciation
/ɑ/	hot	/hɑt/	/b/	boy	/bɔɪ/
	far	/fɑr/	/d/	day	/deɪ/
/æ/	cat	/kæt/	/ʤ/	just	/ʤʌst/
/aɪ/	fine	/faɪn/	/f/	face	/feɪs/
/aʊ/	house	/haʊs/	/g/	get	/gɛt/
/ɛ/	bed	/bɛd/	/h/	hat	/hæt/
/eɪ/	name	/neɪm/	/k/	car	/kɑr/
/i/	need	/nid/	/l/	light	/laɪt/
/ɪ/	sit	/sɪt/	/m/	my	/maɪ/
/oʊ/	go	/goʊ/	/n/	nine	/naɪn/
/ʊ/	book	/bʊk/	/ŋ/	sing	/sɪŋ/
/u/	boot	/but/	/p/	pen	/pɛn/
/ɔ/	dog	/dɔg/	/r/	right	/raɪt/
	four	/fɔr/	/s/	see	/si/
/ɔɪ/	toy	/tɔɪ/	/t/	tea	/ti/
/ʌ/	cup	/kʌp/	/ʧ/	cheap	/ʧip/
/ɛr/	bird	/bɛrd/	/v/	vote	/voʊt/
/ə/	about	/ə'baʊt/	/w/	west	/wɛst/
	after	/'æftər/	/y/	yes	/yɛs/
			/z/	zoo	/zu/
			/ð/	they	/ðeɪ/
			/θ/	think	/θɪŋk/
			/ʃ/	shoe	/ʃu/
			/ʒ/	vision	/'vɪʒən/

Source: *The Newbury House Dictionary plus Grammar Reference*, Fifth Edition, National Geographic Learning/ Cengage Learning, 2014.

RHYTHM

The rhythm of English involves stress and pausing.

Stress

- English words are based on syllables—units of sound that include one vowel sound.

- In every word in English, one syllable has the strongest stress.

- In English, speakers group words that go together based on the meaning and context of the sentence. These groups of words are called *thought groups*. In each thought group, one word is stressed more than the others—the stress is placed on the stressed syllable in this word.

- In general, new ideas and information are stressed.

Pausing

- Pauses in English can be divided into two groups: long and short pauses.

- English speakers use long pauses to mark the conclusion of a thought, items in a list, or choices given.

- Short pauses are used between thought groups to break up the ideas in sentences into smaller, more manageable chunks of information.

INTONATION

English speakers use intonation, or pitch (the rise and fall of their voice), to help express meaning. For example, speakers usually use a rising intonation at the end of *yes/no* questions, and a falling intonation at the end of *wh-* questions and statements.

Presentation Strategies

You will often have to give individual or group presentations in your class. The strategies below will help you to prepare, present, and reflect on your presentations.

PREPARE

As you prepare your presentation:

Consider Your Topic

- *Choose a topic you feel passionate about.* If you are passionate about your topic, your audience will be more interested and excited about your topic, too. Focus on one major idea that you can bring to life. The best ideas are the ones your audience wants to experience.

Consider Your Purpose

- *Have a strong beginning*. Use an effective *hook*, such as a quote, an interesting example, a rhetorical question, or a powerful image to get your audience's attention. Include one sentence that explains what you will do in your presentation and why.

- *Stay focused.* Make sure your details and examples support your main points. Avoid sidetracks or unnecessary information that takes you away from your topic.

- *Use visuals that relate to your ideas.* Drawings, photos, video clips, infographics, charts, maps, slides, and physical objects can get your audience's attention and explain ideas effectively, quickly, and clearly. For example, a photo or map of a location you mention can help your audience picture a place they have never been. Slides with only key words and phrases can help emphasize your main points. Visuals should be bright, clear, and simple.

- *Have a strong conclusion*. A strong conclusion should serve the same purpose as the strong beginning—to get your audience's attention and make them think. Good conclusions often refer back to the introduction, or beginning, of the presentation. For example, if you ask a question in the beginning, you can answer it in the conclusion. Remember to restate your main points, and add a conclusion device such as a question, a call to action, or a quote.

Consider Your Audience

- *Share a personal story*. You can also present information that will get an emotional reaction; for example, information that will make your audience feel surprised, curious, worried, or upset. This will help your audience relate to you and your topic.
- *Use familiar concepts*. Think about the people in your audience. Ask yourself these questions: Where are they from? How old are they? What is their background? What do they already know about my topic? What information do I need to explain? Use language and concepts they will understand.
- *Be authentic (be yourself!)*. Write your presentation yourself. Use words that you know and are comfortable using.

Rehearse

- *Make an outline* to help you organize your ideas.
- *Write notes on notecards*. Do not write full sentences, just key words and phrases to help you remember important ideas. Mark the words you should stress and places to pause.
- *Review the pronunciation skills* in your book. Check the pronunciation of words you are uncertain about with a classmate, a teacher, or in a dictionary. Note and practice the pronunciation of difficult words.
- *Memorize the introduction and conclusion*. Rehearse your presentation several times. Practice saying it out loud to yourself (perhaps in front of a mirror or video recorder) and in front of others.
- *Ask for feedback*. Note and revise material that doesn't flow smoothly based on feedback and on your own performance in rehearsal. If specific words or phrases are still a problem, rephrase them.

PRESENT

As you present:

- Pay attention to your pacing (how fast or slow you speak). Remember to speak slowly and clearly. Pause to allow your audience to process information.
- Speak at a volume loud enough to be heard by everyone in the audience, but not too loud. Ask the audience if your volume is OK at the beginning of your talk.
- Vary your intonation. Don't speak in the same tone throughout the talk. Your audience will be more interested if your voice rises and falls, speeds up and slows down to match the ideas you are talking about.
- Be friendly and relaxed with your audience. Remember to smile!
- Show enthusiasm for your topic. Use humor if appropriate.
- Have a relaxed body posture. Don't stand with your arms folded or look down at your notes. Use gestures when helpful to emphasize your points.
- Don't read directly from your notes. Use them to help you remember ideas.
- Don't look at or read from your visuals too much. Use them to support and illustrate your ideas.
- Use frequent eye contact with the entire audience.

REFLECT

As you reflect on your presentation:

- *Consider what you think went well* during your presentation and what areas you can improve upon.

- *Get feedback* from your classmates and teacher. How do their comments relate to your own thoughts about your presentation? Did they notice things you didn't? How can you use their feedback in your next presentation?

Vocabulary Learning Strategies

Vocabulary learning is an on-going process. The strategies below will help you learn and remember new vocabulary words.

Guessing Meaning from Context

You can often guess the meaning of an unfamiliar word by looking at or listening to the words and sentences around it. Speakers usually know when a word is unfamiliar to the audience, or is essential to understanding the main ideas, and will often provide clues as to its meaning.

- Restatement or synonym: A speaker may give a synonym to explain the meaning of a word, using phrases such as, *in other words, also called, or …, also known as*.

- Antonyms: A speaker may define a word by explaining what it is NOT. The speaker might say *Unlike A / In contrast to A, B is …*

- Definition: Listen for signals such as *which means* or *is defined as*. Definitions can also be signaled by a pause.

- Examples: A speaker may provide examples that can help you figure out what something is. For example, *Paris-Plage is a* **recreation** *area on the River Seine, in Paris, France. It has a sandy beach, a swimming pool, and areas for inline skating, playing volleyball, and other activities.*

Understanding Word Families: Stems, Prefixes, and Suffixes

Use your understanding of stems, prefixes, and suffixes to recognize unfamiliar words and to expand your vocabulary. A stem is the root part of the word, which provides the main meaning.

A prefix is before the stem and usually modifies meaning (e.g., adding *re-* to a word means "again"). A suffix is after the stem and usually changes the part of speech (e.g., adding *–ation / –sion / –ion* to a verb changes it to a noun). For example, in the word *endangered*, the stem or root is *danger*, the prefix is *en–*, and the suffix is *–ed*. Words that share the same stem or root belong to the same word family (e.g., *event, eventful, uneventful, uneventfully*).

Word Stem	Meaning	Example
ann (or *enn*)	year	anniversary, millennium
chron(o)	time	chronological, synchronize
flex (or *flect*)	bend	flexible, reflection
graph	draw, write	graphics, paragraph
lab	work	labor, collaborate
mob	move	mobility, automobile
sect	cut	sector, bisect
vac	empty	vacant, evacuate

Prefix	Meaning	Example
auto-	self	automatic, autonomy
bi-	two	bilingual, bicycle
dis-	not, negation, remove	disappear, disadvantages
inter-	between	Internet, international
mis-	bad, badly, incorrectly	misunderstand, misjudge
pre-	before	prehistoric, preheat
re-	again; back	repeat; return
trans-	across, beyond	transfer, translate

Suffix	Part of Speech	Example
-able (or *-ible*)	adjective	believable, impossible
-en	verb	lengthen, strengthen
-ful	adjective	beautiful, successful
-ize	verb	modernize, summarize
-ly	adverb; adjective	carefully, happily; friendly, lonely
-ment	noun	assignment, statement
-tion (or *-sion*)	noun	education, occasion
-wards	adverb	backwards, forwards

Using a Dictionary

A dictionary is a useful tool to help you understand unfamiliar vocabulary you read or hear. Here are some helpful tips for using a dictionary:

- When you see or hear a new word, try to guess its part of speech (noun, verb, adjective, etc.) and meaning, then look it up in a dictionary.

- Some words have multiple meanings. Look up a new word in the dictionary, and try to choose the correct meaning for the context. Then see if it makes sense within the context.

- When you look up a word, look at all the definitions to see if there is a basic core meaning. This will help you understand the word when it is used in a different context. Also look at all the related words, or words in the same family. This can help you expand your vocabulary. For example, the core meaning of *structure* involves something built or put together.

struc·ture /ˈstrʌktʃər/ *n.* **1** [C] a building of any kind: *A new structure is being built on the corner.* **2** [C] any architectural object of any kind: *The Eiffel Tower is a famous Parisian structure.* **3** [U] the way parts are put together or organized: *the structure of a song∥a business's structure*
—*v.* [T] **-tured, -turing, -tures** to put together or organize parts of s.t.: *We are structuring a plan to hire new teachers.* *-adj.* **structural.**

Source: *The Newbury House Dictionary plus Grammar Reference*, Fifth Edition, National Geographic Learning/ Cengage Learning, 2014.

Multi-Word Units

You can improve your fluency if you learn and use vocabulary as multi-word units: idioms (*mend fences*), collocations (*trial and error*), and fixed expressions (*in other words*). Some multi-word units can only be understood as a chunk—the individual words do not add up to the same overall meaning. Keep track of multi-word units in a notebook or on notecards.

Vocabulary Note Cards

You can expand your vocabulary by using vocabulary note cards. Write the word, expression, or sentence that you want to learn on one side. On the other, draw a four-square grid and write the following information in the squares: definition; translation (in your first language); sample sentence; synonyms. Choose words that are high frequency or on the academic word list. If you have looked a word up a few times, you should make a card for it.

definition:	*first language translation:*
sample sentence:	*synonyms:*

Organize the cards in review sets so you can practice them. Don't put words that are similar in spelling or meaning in the same review set, as you may get them mixed up. Go through the cards and test yourself on the meanings of the words or expressions. You can also practice with a partner.

TED Talk Summary Worksheet

Unit: _____   Video Title: _____

Speaker: _____

What information did you learn about the speaker and his or her background?

_____

_____

_____

What hook does the speaker use?

_____

Summarize the main idea in one sentence.

_____

What was the most interesting part of the talk? What would you tell a friend about it?

_____

_____

_____

How does the speaker engage the audience? (e.g., photos, infographics, other visuals, humor, gestures, personal story)

_____

How does the speaker conclude the talk? (e.g., call to action, question)

_____

What is your opinion of the talk? What words would you use to describe it?

_____

_____

What words or phrases in the talk are new to you? Write three and their definitions.

_____

_____

_____

Presentation Scoring Rubrics

Unit 1

Note: 1= lowest; 5 = highest

The presenter …	Name _____	Name _____	Name _____	Name _____
1. started strong.	1 2 3 4 5	1 2 3 4 5	1 2 3 4 5	1 2 3 4 5
2. clearly explained the purpose of the project.	1 2 3 4 5	1 2 3 4 5	1 2 3 4 5	1 2 3 4 5
3. stressed content words.	1 2 3 4 5	1 2 3 4 5	1 2 3 4 5	1 2 3 4 5
4. concluded by explaining why the project will be helpful.	1 2 3 4 5	1 2 3 4 5	1 2 3 4 5	1 2 3 4 5
Overall Rating	1 2 3 4 5	1 2 3 4 5	1 2 3 4 5	1 2 3 4 5
What did you like?				
What could be improved?				

Unit 2

Note: 1= lowest; 5 = highest

The presenter …	Name _____	Name _____	Name _____	Name _____
1. clearly explained the issue.	1 2 3 4 5	1 2 3 4 5	1 2 3 4 5	1 2 3 4 5
2. explained the causes.	1 2 3 4 5	1 2 3 4 5	1 2 3 4 5	1 2 3 4 5
3. explained the effects.	1 2 3 4 5	1 2 3 4 5	1 2 3 4 5	1 2 3 4 5
4. reduced vowels.	1 2 3 4 5	1 2 3 4 5	1 2 3 4 5	1 2 3 4 5
5. made an emotional connection.	1 2 3 4 5	1 2 3 4 5	1 2 3 4 5	1 2 3 4 5
Overall Rating	1 2 3 4 5	1 2 3 4 5	1 2 3 4 5	1 2 3 4 5
What did you like?				
What could be improved?				

Unit 3

Note: 1= lowest; 5 = highest

The presenter …	Name _____					Name _____					Name _____					Name _____				
1. showed two maps.	1	2	3	4	5	1	2	3	4	5	1	2	3	4	5	1	2	3	4	5
2. described the difference between them.	1	2	3	4	5	1	2	3	4	5	1	2	3	4	5	1	2	3	4	5
3. clearly pronounced *can* and *can't*.	1	2	3	4	5	1	2	3	4	5	1	2	3	4	5	1	2	3	4	5
4. spoke clearly and paused effectively.	1	2	3	4	5	1	2	3	4	5	1	2	3	4	5	1	2	3	4	5
Overall Rating	1	2	3	4	5	1	2	3	4	5	1	2	3	4	5	1	2	3	4	5
What did you like?																				
What could be improved?																				

Unit 4

Note: 1= lowest; 5 = highest

The presenter …	Name _____					Name _____					Name _____					Name _____				
1. asked clear, open questions.	1	2	3	4	5	1	2	3	4	5	1	2	3	4	5	1	2	3	4	5
2. paid attention to the person's answers.	1	2	3	4	5	1	2	3	4	5	1	2	3	4	5	1	2	3	4	5
3. asked follow-up questions.	1	2	3	4	5	1	2	3	4	5	1	2	3	4	5	1	2	3	4	5
4. pronounced numbers correctly.	1	2	3	4	5	1	2	3	4	5	1	2	3	4	5	1	2	3	4	5
Overall Rating	1	2	3	4	5	1	2	3	4	5	1	2	3	4	5	1	2	3	4	5
What did you like?																				
What could be improved?																				

Unit 5

Note: 1= lowest; 5 = highest

The presenter …	Name _____					Name _____					Name _____					Name _____				
1. clearly explained the inspiration for the project.	1	2	3	4	5	1	2	3	4	5	1	2	3	4	5	1	2	3	4	5
2. explained its application.	1	2	3	4	5	1	2	3	4	5	1	2	3	4	5	1	2	3	4	5
3. used signal words to mark transitions.	1	2	3	4	5	1	2	3	4	5	1	2	3	4	5	1	2	3	4	5
4. linked words for smooth speech.	1	2	3	4	5	1	2	3	4	5	1	2	3	4	5	1	2	3	4	5
5. had a strong ending.	1	2	3	4	5	1	2	3	4	5	1	2	3	4	5	1	2	3	4	5
Overall Rating	1	2	3	4	5	1	2	3	4	5	1	2	3	4	5	1	2	3	4	5
What did you like?																				
What could be improved?																				

Unit 6

Note: 1= lowest; 5 = highest

The presenter …	Name _____					Name _____					Name _____					Name _____				
1. presented the agency clearly (roles A, B, C).	1	2	3	4	5	1	2	3	4	5	1	2	3	4	5	1	2	3	4	5
2. responded to questions with appropriate support (roles A, B, C).	1	2	3	4	5	1	2	3	4	5	1	2	3	4	5	1	2	3	4	5
3. was personable (roles A, B, C).	1	2	3	4	5	1	2	3	4	5	1	2	3	4	5	1	2	3	4	5
4. asked appropriate questions (role D).	1	2	3	4	5	1	2	3	4	5	1	2	3	4	5	1	2	3	4	5
5. clearly explained reasons (role D).	1	2	3	4	5	1	2	3	4	5	1	2	3	4	5	1	2	3	4	5
6. spoke in thought groups (all roles).	1	2	3	4	5	1	2	3	4	5	1	2	3	4	5	1	2	3	4	5
Overall Rating (all roles)	1	2	3	4	5	1	2	3	4	5	1	2	3	4	5	1	2	3	4	5
What did you like?																				
What could be improved?																				

Unit 7

Note: 1= lowest; 5 = highest

The presenter …	Name _____	Name _____	Name _____	Name _____
1. used "bookends" to introduce and end presentation.	1 2 3 4 5	1 2 3 4 5	1 2 3 4 5	1 2 3 4 5
2. clearly introduced the situation.	1 2 3 4 5	1 2 3 4 5	1 2 3 4 5	1 2 3 4 5
3. explained its benefits and problems.	1 2 3 4 5	1 2 3 4 5	1 2 3 4 5	1 2 3 4 5
4. offered possible solutions.	1 2 3 4 5	1 2 3 4 5	1 2 3 4 5	1 2 3 4 5
5. used signposts.	1 2 3 4 5	1 2 3 4 5	1 2 3 4 5	1 2 3 4 5
Overall Rating	1 2 3 4 5	1 2 3 4 5	1 2 3 4 5	1 2 3 4 5
What did you like?				
What could be improved?				

Unit 8

Note: 1= lowest; 5 = highest

The presenter …	Name _____	Name _____	Name _____	Name _____
1. clearly introduced the animal and its habitat.	1 2 3 4 5	1 2 3 4 5	1 2 3 4 5	1 2 3 4 5
2. clearly explained the threats the animal faces and possible responses to those threats.	1 2 3 4 5	1 2 3 4 5	1 2 3 4 5	1 2 3 4 5
3. presented an effective visual.	1 2 3 4 5	1 2 3 4 5	1 2 3 4 5	1 2 3 4 5
4. used correct intonation in *wh-* questions.	1 2 3 4 5	1 2 3 4 5	1 2 3 4 5	1 2 3 4 5
Overall Rating	1 2 3 4 5	1 2 3 4 5	1 2 3 4 5	1 2 3 4 5
What did you like?				
What could be improved?				

Vocabulary Index

Credits